YOU DON'T NEED TO
SLAY MY
DRAGONS

Just Take Out the Trash

YOU DON'T NEED TO
SLAY MY
DRAGONS

Just Take Out the Trash

BEVERLY CAMPBELL

DESERET
BOOK

SALT LAKE CITY, UTAH

To Pierce—my friend,
my eternal companion, my hero—
whose armor has never tarnished

Library of Congress Cataloging-in-Publication Data

Campbell, Beverly.
  You don't need to slay my dragons, just take out the trash / Beverly Campbell.
     p. cm.
  ISBN-13: 978-1-59038-862-4 (hardbound : alk. paper)
  1. Man-woman relationships—Religious aspects—Church of Jesus Christ of Latter-day Saints.   2. Sex role—Religious aspects—Church of Jesus Christ of Latter-day Saints.   3. Marriage—Religious aspects—Church of Jesus Christ of Latter-day Saints.   4. Church of Jesus Christ of Latter-day Saints—Doctrines.   I. Title.
  BX8641.C35 2008
  248.4'89332—dc22   2007046817

Printed in the United States of America
Publishers Printing, Salt Lake City, UT

10 9 8 7 6 5 4 3 2 1

CONTENTS

~

SECTION I
OF HEROES AND QUEENS

Acknowledgments

$\sim$

I would like to acknowledge and thank all those who have responded to my questionnaires, participated in discussions, and provided the insights and ideas on which this book is based. I would also like to extend a grateful and specific thanks to Jana Erickson, my product director, and to Emily Watts, my editor, who have afforded invaluable professional guidance in the shaping and finalizing of this effort.

INTRODUCTION

~

Recently my husband, Pierce, and I had dinner with our number-two grandson, Robert. Robert has completed his university degree, is filled with promise, and is exceptional in every way. He's smart, handsome, spiritual, fun, athletic, sensitive and thoughtful. (How amazing to find all these traits in one young man!) Anyone looking at him would say, "There's a guy who has it all figured out."

We were discussing this book and some of the ideas regarding partnerships—and the interesting challenges he was facing as he searched for his own eternal partner. He said to me, "Grandmother, what you're talking about is as important to men as it is to women. Why don't you write this book to all of us?"

That night, as I pondered a nearly completed manuscript directed at identifying the needs of both men and women, but addressed primarily to women, I thought: "He's right, as usual."

The model that God established is one of partnerships—in all things. The whole story of creation, of life on earth, and even of the hereafter is about partnership.

And God gives us such clear patterns to follow. We don't need to have a Ph.D. in marriage and family counseling to see how He created us as male and female, what He intended our relationships to be, and why these differences are gifts intended to bring delight, light, and salvation to us all.

There are pathways on our journey home to heaven that can only be traveled individually. But after a lifetime of listening, caring, researching, compiling, and living in a partnership—after four decades of paying careful attention to the dynamics at work in male-female relationships—I've concluded there are several basic truths in life and in partnerships that we all need to understand and embrace.

Although statistics show that most readers of "relationship books" will be women, I hope that both men and women will share the contents of this book and enjoy positive, light-filled, heart-filled, fun-filled discussions. I also hope that expanded understandings will arise from these discussions, causing each participant to move forward with informed confidence and grand goodwill. I recently used some of the findings from this book in a major presentation to a large area singles conference. It was telling that as many men as women stood in line after the session to ask questions and expound on their own interests.

This book makes use of and builds on what I have come to call "the principle of three." For me, the number *three* seems to be a great simplifying number on which many principles of truth, administration, wisdom, and justice rest.

The idea is simple: rather than make a long list, pare down your thoughts about important changes in your life to the three key things you will work on. As I have explored and applied this principle, I have found that I'm forced to order and articulate my life mission and priorities in the purest and most manageable format. Quite simply, more than three becomes a list, an agenda, a committee—tasks, not missions.

Because I feel this is such an illuminating principle, not only will you find this book divided into three sections, but you will find in each chapter principles of three to define the main point.

I also believe that all books should be living workbooks. The pages should invite you to write your own comments in the margins, and make notes, so that as you read you can explore in your mind's eye *how* you will actually apply the principles in your own very personal journey.

To this end, following is a list of questions on which you may wish to reflect. Also provided is a place to record your answers as you are ready to do so, or you may prefer to write in a separate notebook or journal so you can have more space to elaborate.

Now, I can hear male readers moaning. This isn't something you find natural to do, is it? However, may I suggest that you just give it a try? This kind of exploration is important to the journey we're taking in this book—and in the end you'll be glad you did it. At various points in the book, both men and women will be asked to look at these answers and use them as a jumping-off point for further discussion.

DISCUSSION BREAK

Past

What are the three major choices that have shaped your life?

1.

2.

3.

Present

What are the three things you wish your partner (or proposed partner) understood about you?

1.

2.

3.

Future

What are the relationship/partnership issues you will address this year?

1.

2.

3.

WHO WERE WE
CREATED TO BE?

———

Some years ago my husband and I, while traveling in China, were taken to an extraordinary restaurant in a very old part of Beijing. This restaurant was located in an ancient complex of buildings with eaves tipped up in the Chinese manner, like the prows of Venetian gondolas. They were adorned with an exceptional array of mystical guardian animals. Our route took us down twisting, narrow streets from which emanated unfamiliar and exotic smells and sounds.

At our destination we passed through an enchanting opening called a Moon Gate, and found ourselves in ancient, traditional, symbolic gardens in which stones, water, shrubs, and benches were artfully combined to create an atmosphere of utmost serenity.

There was little time to bask in that beautifully ordered setting, however, as we were quickly escorted into a dimly lit series of rooms. As our eyes adjusted to the light, the sights took our breath away. On the opposing walls of the two major rooms were magnificent murals, each about five feet high and seven feet wide. Even the most cursory glance spoke of the importance of the work and the skill of the artist. We realized immediately that we were seeing works depicting two major events of Creation.

In one mural, a heroic figure was rending the darkness with a bolt of brilliant light. The artist had strewn "matter unorganized" about, suggesting the use of those elements as the world was coming together.

The other mural showed a walled garden, inhabited by two people. Central to that work were a glorious woman and a magnificent tree laden with fruit. It was a peach tree—and near the tree was a monkey.

When I asked to hear the story of these murals, our host said he didn't know much about them, as they dated from another time and belief system. He did say that in that "lore" there was a story of a man from heaven who rends, with light and attendant sound, the darkness separating heaven and earth. This heroic creature was on assignment to create a new world. As to the second mural, he said that it depicted a glorious garden where a majestic woman was created to be a queen and a companion to this man.

I asked about the peach and the monkey. He advised that in their culture a monkey indicated mischief and trickery. As to the peach, that was the mystical fruit believed to contain elements of a spiritual nature. The woman, he told us, needed to eat the peach because she was the one who had to take the next step in the journey of creation—a step equal in importance to rending the darkness. He understood that it was her job to save those waiting to come through that rent veil by giving them bodies.

As I pressed for more information about the two central figures, he said he believed that the depiction of the man as the central figure in the one mural and the woman as the central figure in the other represented the "yin and yang" of Creation, and that in ancient lore, both were heroes.

I have found that variations of this Creation story permeate all cultures, societies, and ages of man. Perhaps it is because the Creation was an event of such astonishing magnificence, and we were so vested in its plan and purpose, that our very DNA has been permanently imprinted with the sights, sounds, and feelings of a world created *for our sakes.* Perhaps it is only as we come to comprehend this story that we can understand who and why we are here and what we are to become.

To truly understand ourselves and our roles as men and women, we need to have a much clearer picture of who Adam and Eve were created to be and therefore who we were created to be. So, although most of this book will be lighter and more practical in nature, I need to take just a few pages to lay a foundation of eternal principles. (A more complete, in-depth discussion of these concepts is available in my book *Eve and the Choice Made in Eden.*)

The Beginning of the Labors

Before the work of the Creation began, there was a war in heaven instigated by Lucifer, who rallied one-third of the hosts of heaven and tried to wrest the throne of God and the destiny of all humankind away from our Father. His intent was to strip all who claimed mortal bodies of their agency. He would take over, and all glory would be his.

Moses records God's reaction to Satan's attempt to usurp the agency of humankind: "Wherefore, because that Satan rebelled against me, and sought to destroy the agency of man, which I, the Lord God, had given him, and also, that I should give unto him mine own power; by the power of mine Only Begotten, I caused that he should be cast down" (Moses 4:3).

Christ, assisted by Adam and by those other two-thirds of the hosts of heaven (including you and me), fought the good, hard, long fight to defeat Satan. Through this exceptional effort, and because of the growth they had made in the heavens, men and women won the right to be agents for God and for themselves. They each earned the right to claim a body in a world where they could show that they could and would grow in all ways. They earned the right to exercise righteous agency, to create families, and to make choices that would allow them to return and claim a greater and more glorious world for their eternal families.

Everyone knows that first "sent one" to Eden was a man called Adam. But before Adam was Adam, he was Michael the Archangel. He had attained a stature and power in the heavens second only to that of Christ, the Firstborn.

Not only was Michael/Adam given an opportunity, serving under Christ, to help plan and bring all the elements together to create our world, but, upon leaving Eden, he and Eve were given this entire earth to explore, cultivate, develop, tame, subdue, and make fruitful. They were to multiply and replenish it.

Adam was given God's holy priesthood with all its powers,

to be used only in humility and righteousness (see Moses 6:67; D&C 121:41–42).

What This Says about Man's Nature

From the story of Creation we understand that men come into this world having pledged to be God's righteous warriors, with extraordinary allegiance to the world that they have helped Him create. They come with clear priesthood assignments and unambiguous leadership and partnership responsibilities.

From this we can also gather that deep in men's souls is an understanding that the battle is not over. Although Satan's plans for the overthrow of heaven were thwarted, the contest for the minds and souls of all who now inhabit, will inhabit, or ever have inhabited this mortal world has simply changed venues. Men's battle is to tame Satan, to tame the elements, and to tame themselves.

Inherent in that assignment, we can envision a charge to chart the rivers, cross the oceans, and climb the mountains; to discover the uses of the earth and the richness that is hidden therein.

Enter Woman

Next we are introduced to Eve—magnificent, wise, majestic Eve. Elder Bruce R. McConkie wrote: "There is no language that can do credit to our glorious mother Eve. . . . [She] was among the noble and great in preexistence. She ranked in spiritual stature, in faith and devotion, in conformity to eternal law with Michael" ("Eve and the Fall," 68, 67). He speaks of her rejoicing in her foreordination to be the first woman, the mother of men, the consort, companion, and friend of mighty Michael.

Speaking of the creative work that Christ and Michael presided over, Elder McConkie asks: "Can we do other than conclude that Mary and Eve and Sarah and myriads of our faithful sisters were numbered among them?" He goes on to assure, "Certainly these sisters labored as diligently then, and fought as valiantly in the war in heaven, as did the brethren, even as they in like manner stand firm today, in mortality, in the cause of truth and righteousness" (ibid., 59).

Let's look at how we are introduced to Eve in the Bible. Biblical scholars have long established that the first word used to describe this first woman was *ezer*. This word is a combination of two root words. The first root means "to rescue" and "to save," as a savior, or literally, as a lifesaver. This word is used only a few times in the Bible, and in those instances it speaks of God and is used when your need for God to be your helper, your partner, your lifesaver is absolute—when His support is essential to your going on. This root is used in Deuteronomy 33:26 to speak of the God who rides on the heavens to help you. The second root of *ezer* means an unusual strength, unbending (like iron) yet with the ability to bend and not break (like the willow). The word itself is most often combined with majesty (see Freedman, "Woman: A Power Equal to Man," 56).

K'enegdo, another word used in Genesis to describe Eve, is harder to interpret, as it is used only once. Biblical scholar David Freedman states that the late rabbinical commentaries translated the word as "equal" (ibid.).

Suppose we had all, male and female alike, been taught to

understand Genesis 2:18 with its true intent? Perhaps that passage would then read something like this: *"It is not good that man should be alone. I will make him a companion of majesty and strength, who brings with her a saving power and is equal with him."*

Collectively and individually, if humankind had interpreted this scripture in this manner, attitudes, laws, and customs might have been different, and the relationships that God intended between men and women, between husband and wife, between women and society might have been more universally equitable.

We discern from Eve's name and title that she was designed not only to be life-giving but to be lifesaving. Here is a woman filled with a love so great that it extends to all the children hanging over heaven's banisters. Those spirits (including all of us) could not claim bodies and therefore advance in their own journeys unless she made the correct choice, exercised her agency, and took the step necessary for them to claim mortal bodies.

The Fall

We learn that the Fall was foreordained: "Adam and Eve . . . did the very thing that the Lord intended them to do. If we had the original record, we would see the purpose of the fall clearly stated and its necessity explained," taught President Joseph Fielding Smith (*Answers to Gospel Questions*, 4:80).

As to Adam and Eve's "transgression," or their crossing over to mortality, Elder Dallin H. Oaks teaches us that "her [Eve's] act, whatever its nature, was formally a transgression but eternally a glorious necessity to open the doorway toward eternal life. Adam showed his wisdom by doing the same. And thus Eve and Adam fell that men might be" ("Great Plan of Happiness," 73).

We can understand this better as we ponder the Lord's command to them to multiply and replenish the earth, and that He follows the command about eating the fruit of the tree with words used in no other commandment: "Nevertheless, thou mayest choose for thyself" (Moses 3:17).

Unless blood flowed in the veins of Adam and Eve, they would have no children, yet with blood flowing in their veins they could not remain in the rarified atmosphere of Eden. The paradox of being commanded not to partake of rhe forbidden fruit but at the same time to *multiply* had to be reconciled.

The Fruit

Elder Bruce R. McConkie taught: "What is meant by partaking of the fruit of the tree of the knowledge of good and evil is that our first parents complied with whatever laws were involved so that their bodies would change from their state of paradisiacal immortality to a state of natural mortality" ("Christ and the Creation," 15). Neither the tree nor the fruit of the tree had power in themselves to give mortal life. Only God has authority to confer such life.

Eve recognized that the tree and the fruit, both powerful symbols, were also essential gifts of mortal life. She was caused to step back, reevaluate, and *see* that it must be so. The word used to describe this thought process is *beguiled*. A scholar who grew up speaking ancient Hebrew says that this is one of the most multilayered and rich of all biblical words and is so difficult to articulate correctly that it has been tainted in our modern interpretations of that ancient language: "The use of this word would indicate that Eve was motivated by a complex set of inner drives, anchored not only in her physical, but also in her intellectual nature" (Aschkenasy, *Eve's Journey*, 42).

Satan sought to trick or fool Eve and therefore gain control over the bodies and minds of mortals. However, not knowing "the mind of God" (Moses 4:6), he actually became the catalyst that caused her to make this evaluation, call on all her senses, and exercise her agency to partake of the fruit.

What This Says about Woman's Nature

Throughout this story we see that discernment—the ability to see beyond the literal to the divine essential—has ever been God's gift to women. Eve's strength, courage, and intellect are evident, as are her love, her ability to love, and her concern for all the family of man.

It is clear from this that woman's greatest role is to make use of her divine discernment to act in concert with her God and His purposes. She is to help waiting spirits claim mortal bodies. Her nature is designed to hold the family of humankind together—and she is willing to do so at any cost.

Bottom line: As we understand that Eve courageously, heroically, and with enormous generosity of spirit claimed that most precious aspect of agency, the right to exercise spiritual and personal integrity, we begin to see better how women are designed.

This brief overview of the Creation and our first parents is the springboard for our understanding of men and women in our complicated latter days.

SECTION I

OF HEROES AND QUEENS

———

Nothing in life is to be feared.
It is only to be understood.
—MADAME MARIE CURIE

CHAPTER 1

Understanding the Design, Embracing the Differences

~

Since the beginning of modern thought, science has been trying to explain the why and how of the design of men's and women's brains. Early literature suggested the differences to be so far-reaching that women were barred from many meaningful activities, while men were allocated key roles considered to be of import to the community.

Conversely, mid-twentieth-century dialogue directed us to the belief that men and women are essentially the same in all but childbearing. Researchers and others wrote, taught, and seemed to sincerely believe that any differences in feelings, actions, likes, and dislikes could be explained away as the result of our orientation or our acculturation.

Both views were based on information available at that time—and I'm sure it comes as no surprise to you that both were seriously flawed. Amazing leaps forward in technology have allowed scientists to examine the brain in ways never before possible. And science has made some exciting and helpful findings regarding our amazing and different "divine" brain designs.

Science has now shown objectively what most thinking men and women have known all along: Men's and women's brains, thought processes, and intuitive responses are quite different, just as were Adam's and Eve's. A study cited in *Nature*, a scientific journal of some stature, suggests that women's brains are much more complex than ever thought. The researchers also found that men's brain activity remains basically the same from day to day and is fairly simple.

A Duke University genome expert and one of the authors of the study articulated it this way: "Genetically speaking, if you've met one man, you've met them all. We are, I hate to say it, predictable. You can't say that about women. Men and women are farther apart than we ever knew . . . and women's brains are much more complex than we ever imagined" (as quoted in Dowd, "Genetically Speaking").

> *"Men and women are farther apart than we ever knew . . . and women's brains are much more complex than we ever imagined."*

Such broad statements made me want to understand more clearly what his research had uncovered. It seems that our main differences are linked to the fact that men have only 45 chromosomes with which to do their work. In this male expert's words: "Our 46th is the pathetic Y that has only a few genes which operate below the waist and above the knees." He then went on to note that women have the full 46 chromosomes, and the 46th is a second X "that is working at levels greater than we knew" (ibid.).

Those researchers believe that men and women really do think differently because of actual physiological differences. Those differences seem to have much more to do with nature (God's design) than nurture (human shaping).

David Page, a molecular biologist and expert on evolution, writes that the male Y chromosome is the blank slate on which men can blame almost anything. Perhaps that chromosome carries the "inability to remember birthdays and anniversaries" gene, the "fascination with spiders and reptiles" gene, the "selective hearing loss, or 'Huh?'" gene, and the "inability to express affection on the phone" gene. It may well explain why men have trouble expressing themselves when it comes to emotions—their genes just haven't prepared them to do so (ibid.).

Another researcher, Simon Baron-Cohen of Cambridge University, noted that within twenty-four hours after birth a baby boy will focus on a mobile, a baby girl on a face. Even this early in life, studies thus demonstrate some of the "interpersonal detachment and mechanical interest" of males versus the "desire to read people" interest of females (see "They Just Can't Help It").

The linear thought process of males has value, as it keeps them focused on the immediate task and allows them to block out extraneous distractions. Their job as hunter-provider often calls for this. Unfortunately this also allows them to block out the baby crying, the children scuffling, and the doorbell ringing.

A woman's thought processes move her easily into the networking that signals concern for the greatest good for the greatest number in her caring circle. It seems that women are ever aware of and processing people, events, and responsibilities. Because women's brains work in a networking pattern, they are, as a general rule, consummate multitaskers. They can sort out a variety of voices and needs and include many people in a series of conversations all going on at the same time. They often have several projects going and effortlessly change from one to another.

This drives my husband (and most men I know) crazy. They don't understand how you can be preparing dinner, helping Susie with her homework, monitoring what Jim is doing on the computer, talking on the telephone with a friend, and still hear what they are saying.

Pierce will say, "Stop and just listen to me." I can repeat back every word that he has said, along with the intent of those words, and he still doesn't believe I was listening unless that's *all* I was doing. Men's brains actually may not work in this networking way, so they may have no frame of reference for such ability.

These theories direct us to an understanding of why guys are so good at visual and spatial things like hitting fast-moving balls or making mental maps or compulsively playing and winning at table hockey and X-Box games. It turns out that the focus part of the brain and the ability to shut out all else—which underpins those skills—is apparently much more dominant in men than in women (see Hales, "The Female Brain," 172–84).

It's important to factor into this discussion an awareness that no two men are exactly alike any more than any two women are alike. Supposing you were measuring on a scale from 1 to 10—with 1 being alpha male and 10 being omega female. Some men will be at the extreme 1 end of the "male-ness" scale, while others will be much nearer the 5, where awareness and sensitivities move closer to their female counterparts. Most, however, are somewhere between 1 and 5. The same is true for women. Some are going to be at the 6, and they think and respond more similarly to their male counterparts, while others will be at the extreme 10 and respond to almost everything in an extremely "female" way.

I am often surprised that the idea of women being different from men is offensive to some. To relegate woman's role to that of carbon copy is to assign her to be forever second class. Such assignment denies all that is strong and noble in the unique contributions a woman brings to life. Her thought processes, her talents and abilities, while of equal value, are not the same as those of men.

The reality is that opportunities in every field should be as open to women as they are to men. There should be equal educational opportunities, equal sports programs, and equal pay for equal work. Career choices should be equally open, and respect should be equally accorded for a woman's life choices. However, there is a difference between the genders, and that difference is divine in origin. Unless we understand that design, we likely will not value the distinction.

While science has proven that men's and women's brains are, indeed, configured differently, it is important to understand that neither configuration is more valid—they are just different.

This brings us to that "other" with whom you're trying to communicate. Many are puzzled by their inability to find or retain common ground with the opposite sex in daily personal or business interactions. Partners are bewildered when experiences aren't internalized in the same way, when language doesn't mean the same thing, when often their reactions to the same event are different. Yet, we know that as individuals we've had a lifetime of experiences and reactions that are quite different from the experiences and reactions of others. So, why are we surprised when words, sights, and sounds don't mean the same thing to the two sharing the incident? Even if our experiences have been similar, we have processed them quite differently. In truth, no one can ever share the same experience exactly.

In truth, no one can ever share the same experience exactly.

The ways in which men and women see and process things such as emotions, voice tones, and body language are more dissimilar than similar. Because of this, words, when spoken, don't evoke the same images. Women's brains tend to lead them to an instinctive feel for the meaning behind the words, utilizing a whole spectrum of emotions. Men's brains seem to be looking for the logic of the matter, and mostly they just get "blips," similar to those a control tower's radar picks up when there is something in the flight path that isn't close enough to identify. From our earliest years, there is very little in life that we do not process and internalize differently.

Add to that the fact that no two people learn to communicate, plan, solve problems, or even have fun in the same way, and you no longer have to ask, "Why aren't we finding common ground?" The question now is, "How *do* we find common ground, and how do we build on that common ground once we've found it?"

There is no right way to be or to respond. What we'll talk about in the following chapters are general, "heads-up" ideas, so you can recognize tendencies and not always be mystified, confused, or hurt by the reaction of the "other."

CHAPTER 2

THREE THINGS MEN WOULD LIKE WOMEN TO KNOW ABOUT THEM

⸺

Have you noticed that there are few little boys who do not see the sword as an extension of their arm and their supremacy, who do not attempt to turn a twig, or a bar of soap, or their hand, into a gun, whether or not they have ever been allowed to play with toy guns?

Have you noticed that as soon as a boy child is introduced to a spoon, he ferrets it out to the backyard where it becomes an instrument of exploration as he seeks to tunnel to China?

Have you noticed that boys instinctively race to the top of any rise in the landscape to claim it by right and title as king, where they will defend said "hill" against all comers?

Have you noticed that boys, large and small, secretly believe they possess superhuman powers—powers that they test over and over, regardless of consequence? At age one and a half they jump from atop the back of the couch, at three from a tree, at six off the odd roof, at eight from the banned skateboard ramp, at twelve from the cliff to raging water below. Have you noticed that this "jumping" (labeled by some as risk taking) continues until their very late adult years?

Recently, I came across a reference to an ad which seemed designed to elicit no response at all. It read:

MEN WANTED FOR HAZARDOUS JOURNEY.
Small wages, bitter cold, long months of complete dark-
ness, constant danger, safe return doubtful. Honor and
recognition in case of success.

That ad, placed in London newspapers in 1900, was in preparation for the National Antarctic Expedition. Ernest Shackleton, the leader of the expedition, later said of this call for volunteers: "It seemed as though all the men in Great Britain were determined to accompany me, the response was so overwhelming" (as quoted in Bennett, *Book of Virtues*, 493).

What Men Tell Us about This

As part of the preparation for this chapter I conducted a poll among a number of men to learn some of the things men wish women understood about them. The sampling was large, the ages varied, the occupations and life experiences diverse. When the findings were compiled and condensed into general traits, I discovered that men truly do see themselves as they were created to be—and that is who they've been trying to be since escaping from the crib.

1. Men see themselves as heroes, righteous warriors, and intrepid adventurers. Bravery in general, however, is not enough; they want to be *personal* heroes to their own beloved queens and families. They want to have offspring, and they feel driven to create a world in which those within their influence can thrive.

Why would this come as a surprise to anyone? That is who men were hardwired to be. We talked in the Prologue of their valiant fight as defenders of the great plan of happiness. They waged battle against one-third of the hosts of heaven and were victorious! This victory brought with it a specific assignment, to help in the creation of a world where spirit children of our Heavenly Father could receive mortal bodies, be tested, and gain knowledge—a world where those mortals would receive opportunities to claim the ordinances necessary to return in glory to their heavenly home.

It was the day before God rested that he put his hand to the creation of woman. It was she who was to be the man's partner through it all. It was she who called upon Adam to awaken to the waiting world. Adam realized that without her, all that had gone before would have been just an interesting exercise; with her, their grand adventure could begin.

For her, for the family it was his mission to help create, and for this new world, he could seek honor and do justice. He could be the instrument for initiating and exercising that system of righteous government which ruled the heavens. He could bring the promised blessing of that priesthood to rest on the heads of his beloveds individually and on the family of man collectively.

Deep in a man's soul is the knowledge that he will never realize his greatest fulfillment if he is content to fight the world's battles solely. At that core level, most men understand that the most important and most exciting war they will ever be engaged in is the one that will help establish God's kingdom on earth, for that is the specific battle they came to earth to win.

Perhaps that is why, thankfully, there will always be glorious young men at their very prime ready to give up all worldly possessions and pleasures to devote two years of focused, uninterrupted time to the Lord's work. Perhaps that is why God designed the missionary program that way, for through this process young men learn what it means to be courageous, noble, sensitive, refined, "righteous warriors." During this time they learn what it means to love with the pure love of Christ, to "bring in the sheaves" for his sake. They discover what the refiner's fire is all about.

Deep in a man's soul is the knowledge that he will never realize his greatest fulfillment if he is content to fight the world's battles solely.

All of the above was brought home to me with the receipt of a much-anticipated e-mail from our grandson Matthew, serving a mission in the Philippines. I quote in part: "I have been learning a lot each day about how the Spirit of the Lord works . . . a lot about how charity and our motives are almost directly correlated to the involvement of the Spirit. . . . And that is a reason why contention is such a huge obstacle in this work, as it directly blocks our ability to empathize and emote our love for those we teach."

What an incredible journey with the Spirit—what an amazing training ground!

Perhaps this desire of men to be righteous warriors also explains why there will always be "Men from La Mancha" fighting for good and right and justice wherever they are in the world, whatever their beliefs.

Understanding that soul desire may also help us understand why so many men are drawn to the battles of the world, the games of winning things, yet are never satisfied with what they've won. Some men I surveyed spoke of occasionally feeling stirrings deep inside that caused them to wonder if what they were doing was worth the effort. Some expressed that at times of crisis in their lives, whether emotional, professional, or political, they have questioned whether the prize they were striving for would be worth the cost. Others spoke of their awareness that there were grander battles calling out to them, more meaningful than those they were finding in their workaday world.

In both their daytime flights of fancy and their nighttime dreams, men see themselves as capable of stopping the world from spinning into chaos. They can save planets and people and their families—and fly without wings.

Maybe the "intrepid adventurer" in men is what triggers their seemingly insatiable drive to watch TV shows featuring battles or monster trucks or climbing, running, crawling, flying creatures—along with any program that explores the depths of the jungles, the seven wonders of the ancient world, or alien ships landing. Perhaps it is men's fear of missing some valuable piece of information that causes them to switch from one channel to the other with breakneck speed, hardly allowing others' eyes to focus before the scene changes.

Could our awareness of men's true "spiritual DNA" cast positive insight into their drive to sally forth on hiking, biking, hunting, fishing, climbing, diving, spelunking, or other adventures? Maybe it helps us understand why the movie *Braveheart* was one of the most popular films of all time for men, and why they can watch *Tora! Tora! Tora!* or *The Longest Day* over and over again.

2. Men often see their worth in the way they perform—in their work, in their Church duties, in sports. They also measure their performance by their things—their cars, their toys. They like to keep count, to take stock, so often they're driven by a need to acquire and possess.

Like it or not, a woman is one of the things a man is "counting." You're on his arm because he wants you to be there. Men generally think their wives or girlfriends are wonderful and beautiful, and they don't feel any great need to express that because they assume you already know it. However, because they are essentially visual creatures, they like you to sparkle and shine. Most men want having you on their arm to strike envy in the hearts of other men.

Is all this counting any wonder? Adam was given the assignment to dress and keep the Garden, to name every living creature. He was sent forth from Eden to till the ground, to earn his bread by the sweat of his brow (see Moses 3:15, 19; 4:25, 29). And all this has purpose—that men might subdue the world and provide for themselves and their families in all ways.

Men generally want to provide for their wives and families. In that process, it's important that as women we see them as they see themselves: as our heroes; the strong, brilliant warriors who go out and battle for us every day. They want us to see their day's work as their gift to us and to our family, and they relish a "thanks" when they return home after a hard day—or for almost any task they do, even if it is what they should be doing without being asked. As the women in their lives, we need to recognize that this validation, expressed through admiration in word and look and action, is as important to them as oxygen.

Several men noted that down deep they live with fear that they won't measure up in some way—and they need to be told that they do. One man noted that part of the bravado he displays of being able to take on anything comes from a fear that his inadequacies will be uncovered.

Another man noted that, if they aren't quite sure whether they're up to it, many men may reject out of hand a new experience or challenge proposed by the women in their lives. They prefer to decide themselves what "tests" they want to take on. This man said that men don't like to look foolish or be perceived as having failed—particularly by women. Another noted that men sometimes are quite surprised when they pass whatever they perceive the "test" to be with flying colors. He asked if I had ever noticed how often men use phrases such as "I just lucked out," or "I really pulled that one off."

Some men also noted that, in love and relationship issues, their egos often lead them to put a woman to the test first—the woman will be forced to prove she loves the man, needs him, wants him, and admires him. If the woman doesn't rise to the test, he can retreat with his ego and emotions intact. He doesn't often think of the longer-term effects of such an action on the relationship; at the moment it's about protecting a fairly fragile ego. This trait in moderation is all right and even fairly natural. If both men and women are aware of it, they can recognize how to act with greater sensitivity. In excess, however, these ego needs should set off all kinds of alarm bells. Some men, when feeling threatened, will allow this "putting their woman to the test" to escalate into emotional abuse or even domestic violence.

Many men indicated that they would like it if their wives or girlfriends were to support their intellectual interests along with their basketball and golf, skiing and hunting. But men's linear thought process often leaves them so self-focused that they don't realize, and therefore have to be reminded in positive ways, that other lives and interests need to be similarly supported.

Learn to find the true meaning of the compliments or the love that is expressed in masculine words and deeds.

Although part of a man's sense of worth is tied up in being a perfect partner, most men have different ideas from those of most women about what makes a perfect partner. Women: their grand gestures will likely be couched in their own language and actions rather than in yours. So don't be offended when they don't use flowery language or act as sensitively as you would like. Learn to find the true meaning of the compliments and see the love that is expressed in masculine words and deeds.

For men, loving physical touch is a powerful and effective way of affirming their worth. A hug, a kiss, a hand on the shoulder, the promise of a rendezvous can do much to open that part of the brain that validates them and opens lines of communication.

The men in my survey expressed how important physical love is to them. They need to have physical love and want to be the perfect lover—and they want to be told *how* to be that to their wives. One respondent noted that men tend to treat women in life and in lovemaking the way *they* want to be treated—and women do the same. He suggested that what spouses need to do is "get over themselves," and each treat the other the way that other wants to be treated. Each needs to honestly, sensitively, and openly articulate what works for him or her, and then to listen to, believe, and act on the spouse's input.

Part of men's sense of self is that they quite like themselves as they are. They don't want to be changed, fixed, or fine tuned. As to looks, they may see "bulk" as manly, so trying to get them to diet generally doesn't work, unless you can tie it to helping them win the next race.

Men often see bald as bad and would prefer that you don't discuss hair loss or anything about their looks, except that they look "manly." However, a few friendly suggestions slipped in at just the right time may be accepted. Mostly you can probably get by with just telling him if a tie is required, and encourage him not to revert to caveman dress for casual outings.

Unless he asks—or you deem it essential to his next promotion—don't advise a man in jobs or etiquette beyond the necessary basics. He may not like being reminded of those basics, but he won't relish looking too crude or unmannered in crucial situations, either.

Men accept (some more than others) the need to act in a civilized manner. However, they have a deep-seated, almost visceral reaction to being "tamed." You see, deep inside every man is the knowledge that he is to be tamed only by his real General, his Savior—for whom he will fight and to whom he will accede. Men are His warriors; it is His kingdom.

Have you not marveled at the change in the nature of a man, his actions and words, when he truly embraces the priesthood of God and agrees to serve that God? One of the great spiritual moments of my life occurred at an event where hundreds of young men in white shirts and ties marched down the aisles singing: "Called to serve Him, heav'nly King of glory, Chosen e'er to witness for his name." This triumphant march of righteous warriors ended with these words: "God our strength will be; press forward ever, Called to serve our King" (*Hymns*, 249). Yes, that is who men are at their core.

It is always enlightening to see how God balances his scales: While men are sent to tame and bring justice, women are sent to civilize and to create a climate where mercy has equal weight with justice.

It is always enlightening to see how God balances his scales: While men are sent to tame and bring justice, women are sent to civilize and to create a climate where mercy has equal weight with justice. These are two equally important roles that need recognition, validation, and support one from the other.

3. Men generally asserted that facts trump feelings—that they're more responsive to facts than feelings. And although most men relate more easily to facts, many reluctantly noted that they do feel deeply. They care intensely about those they love and have a real depth of spirituality that serves as their anchor.

Many men commented on how emotionally dependent they are on the women in their lives, and how they are affected at both an empathetic and a sympathetic level by the feelings of those women. They also noted that because they have been discouraged from being in touch with their emotions from a very early age, they often would rather not acknowledge that they are affected—much less talk about it. But they do notice and they do care.

Men often experience the same emotional ups and downs as women; they just aren't driven to explore them and have been trained to cover them up.

When it comes to spirituality, men often want to talk about the basics and the philosophy of their spirituality and are sometimes a bit uncomfortable when women speak in their language of the feelings of the Spirit. Some noted that they need a steady awareness and reminder of their priesthood, with its attendant purpose, power, and responsibilities, to serve as compass and check.

As to emotions, the fact that men don't always respond outwardly to moments of emotion does not mean they don't feel them as deeply as women do. Men often experience the same emotional ups and downs as women; they just aren't driven to explore them and have been trained to cover them up. They feel good when women—not always, but on occasion—make the effort to open what is hidden in their hearts. Some saw that as a kind of permission to express their emotions more clearly.

One man said: "Don't ask me what I'm thinking, because I'm probably not thinking much. Do ask me how I'm feeling, because I'm always feeling something." Another suggested: "After you ask me what I'm feeling, give me the space to express that feeling in my own language, using my own frame of reference." You see, women tend to jump in with their great empathy and say "I know what you mean" or "I think what you're feeling is . . ." without giving the man the time he needs to identify and put words to his feelings. Women, be patient, and be prepared—what he's going to tell you may very likely not be what you're feeling or what you think he should be feeling. You wanted to know *his* feelings and you asked—now validate.

Men do cry; they just cry at different times and for different reasons than you do, and more often when they are alone. There are reasons for this and they have to do with control (fear of losing it) and upbringing ("boys don't cry").

Generally, however, rather than talk of thoughts or feelings, men would rather do something like turn the television a bit louder, or go out and hammer on something, or shoot hoops. Some have a real problem with admitting or showing that they have been touched by a scene, a word, an emotion. Even if they're not very good at gazing at the sunset and whispering sweet nothings, the one thing most men noted was that the woman in their life is their primary anchor, their greatest influence, and the reason they get up in the morning and come home at night.

DISCUSSION BREAK

Men, here's where the exercise from the front of the book applies. Identify those three things you wish your wife or sweetheart knew about you specifically and discuss them with her. Women, your task at this point is to listen without interrupting.

CHAPTER 3

OFFSHOOT TRAITS

~

Women who are trying to sort out relationships with men often ask: "Why do so many personal interactions come across as 'I win—you lose' dialogues when our goal should be mutual winning?" The answer is simple, say many psychologists:

1. Most men think in terms of win and lose; don't take it personally.

Men are often motivated by that hero/warrior concept of winning and losing, and in this mind-set they become very self-focused, rather than other- or couple-focused. Add to that the linear thought process of most men's brains, which generally doesn't engage in a network focus, and you can see why winning in its various forms becomes a natural desire for men. Can't you see it as you watch boys at play? This gamesmanship often continues from childhood through old age, in business or at home.

The knockdowns or "gotcha's" are not intended to be taken personally. It started in their first forts or clubhouses as part of their friendship exchanges: "I know more stats than you do." "I have more baseball cards than you." "I'm better than you because I really beat you at . . . [you fill in the game]." Do you know of many men, no matter their age, who will give an inch in a game of tennis or chess or Monopoly? Of course not—it's against their principles, whatever that means.

Now, my children will tell you I don't give much in a game either. The desire to win is quite universal. Women's approaches and intensity in the process, however, tend to be less dominant, less "gotcha."

A word of caution: Men indicated they aren't all that pleased when you, as their partner, place yourself in competition with them. They noted that even when this is done lovingly, they will likely revert to "guy rules"—which means "no holds barred" and "winner take all." If you're willing to compete on that basis—let the games begin.

The fact that many men are driven by concepts of winning, that they want to succeed, that they want to be decision makers, is not necessarily bad. It fits with their being out in the world every day as providers and producers. Women can tap into this trait in positive terms without giving up anything of themselves.

For example, try seeing your man as your hero, the literal "king of the hill." Use sincere phrases that appeal to his best instincts: "How wonderful that you know how to do this." "I'm so glad to have your help." "It's fortunate you're able to see this through." What man alive wouldn't want to bask in such focused light?

The other side of this language issue is that men don't process language in the same way women do. So if you want your husband to empty the garbage, take you to the movies, or get you a drink, say exactly that—not, "Would you . . ." or "What do you think about . . ." or "I'm thirsty." In the logic of a man's factoid-centered mind, those are not requests because they contain no declarative call to action.

Professionals who deal with relationship issues suggest that words translate into action for men only if you make them action statements—which is against women's more relationship-sensitive nature, but in tune with men's ability to hear. So try statements like: "I want to eat at this restaurant so pull into the parking lot right here." "Please take the garbage out now." "We've been wanting to play golf together, so I've checked your schedule and our tee time is set for . . ." Your language needs to be clear, unambiguous, and declarative—not bossy—if you are to get your message across.

This direct form of communication is essential, say many psychologists, if a woman really wants something done and doesn't want to have her feelings hurt all the time by what seems like neglect or lack of caring on her husband's part.

One woman said to me, "Whenever my husband suggests he wants something, I tell him to get it and to buy the very best, because that's what I want him to tell me when I express a need or a desire for something." After thirty years, he still hasn't picked up on that hint. But she insists that she can't communicate more directly with him, because it will only mean something to her if he acts on his own. Don't fall into this trap! Give the men in your life a break. Speak to them in a language they can understand. They weren't programmed for subtle innuendo or for mind reading.

Another aspect of a man's linear thought process is his tendency to believe, "I made it happen." Even the most casual observer notes that men do believe that they hung the stars and the moon (and perhaps they did). However, this belief can be one of their less attractive traits, as it often leads men to take credit for everything anyone does within their sphere of influence—particularly those things women do.

Come on, guys, who do you think designed the stars, making each one different so they would all feel "special"? Who proposed that the moon be filled with rills and valleys that, when viewed from earth, would create the appearance of a face, to the delight of earth's children?

Who do you think collected all the materials needed to get the project finished, reminded you that the job really needed to be done "now," got the stepladder out, held it, handed you the tools needed to hang those stars securely, stayed by your side until the job was done, and then thanked you for doing it?

All kidding aside, many women have spoken of how they are hurt and perplexed by this dynamic. Too often a woman in a home, business, or Church setting sees the authority male usurp and take credit for projects or events that, from conception to execution, were competently and fully handled by her.

Although it is often done unconsciously, unrighteously owning accomplishments and failing to accord proper recognition erodes future trust and cooperation. Such behaviors can harm the soul of both the one who does the work and the one who claims credit for another's efforts.

Men, be aware of this and make a conscious effort to assess

and recognize verbally and truthfully the efforts and contributions of others, paying particular attention to the enormous contributions of the women in your sphere.

Women, if you find this ownership of your accomplishments happening to you on a regular basis, it is important that you speak up. Clearly and graciously assert, without deference in voice, mannerisms, or body language, that you are grateful for their support of *your* project, and glad you were able to bring it to a successful conclusion (or whatever). As you pleasantly, and with cool control, articulate the facts of the situation, a different climate will likely emerge.

2. A man does want to "slay your dragons"—particularly if you let him know there are dragons in your life.

Another interesting dynamic in understanding male-female relationships is the way each partner views and deals with frustrations and challenges. Often, at the end of the day, all a woman wants to do is to put a task, challenge, or problem into better perspective by verbalizing it, thus venting a few frustrations to a sympathetic fellow traveler. She's not asking for specific actions to be taken.

Men, bless their hearts, want to "slay the dragon" for you. They feel compelled to provide you with a solution. If you don't

> *Often, at the end of the day, all a woman wants to do is to put a task, challenge, or problem into better perspective by verbalizing it, thus venting a few frustrations to a sympathetic fellow traveler. She's not asking for specific actions to be taken.*

accept their suggestions, they often distance themselves, grumbling, "If you didn't want me to fix it, why did you tell me about it in the first place?"

A marriage therapist I asked about this wrote that it is very confusing to men to have you tell them something's wrong that you don't want them to fix. He noted that a man's natural instinct (remember, he wants to be your hero and protector) is: "If someone has hurt or offended you, tell me, and I will hurt them back." My therapist friend suggested that women use one of these directives up front:

1. "I need your help solving this problem, so when we're finished talking about it, you can get to work."

2. "I would appreciate your opinion and input as long as you don't care whether or not I use it."

3. "Please shut up and listen, nod understandingly from time to time, but don't try to solve, fix, educate, or direct. Just listen and be emotionally present. Then please follow up as instructed: (a) Hold me, (b) Just sit by me and don't mention it unless I change your job to option one or two, or (c) Bring chocolates and ice cream."

Men aren't that different in this regard. Unless they ask specifically for help, there are few who want you to attempt to solve their problems or indeed to help them out in any way. Consider the old cliché that one of life's truly unforgivable offenses is to suggest, even when he is definitely lost and an hour late, that he ask for directions. The hunter always knows how to get back to the cave—or wherever it is he's going. He's got a built-in compass in his head, hasn't he?

There is actually some scientific truth in the notion that men have a better built-in compass than women. Women's navigational devices tend to be images. A woman may not know the name of the street, or whether it's a left or a right turn, but she can see in her mind's eye the old church steeple, the big oak, the white building, and so on, and thus she arrives at where she wants to be (see Hales, "The Female Brain," 176). Should this all fail to work, women generally ask for directions sooner rather than later. Both thought processes will generally get you there.

3. When conflicts arise, men usually want space, whereas women want verbal understanding.

A perplexed young wife was struggling to understand why her husband so often physically distanced himself from problems and situations that they needed to solve together. Anyone who has been even a casual observer of male-female relationships knows that when problems arise, men generally prefer to remove themselves and hie off to a safe place, while women want to stay where they are and talk the problem through.

The following scenario played itself out in my own home recently. My husband and I had been involved in an ongoing series of business conferences. We were negotiating on an issue of some consequence and were concerned as matters moved forward that there was some difference between what we were hearing and what the particular person could deliver. However, at the conclusion of the conference, which had taken place in our home, Pierce quietly picked up a book and went to his den, closing the door.

It has taken me a number of years to understand what this means and why it is all right. Aware of that basic law of nature, "Don't beard a lion in his den," but needing to talk this through, I went to my study. After I had organized my thoughts, I pressed the telephone's intercom button and asked my husband what he thought had really been the intent of the words and actions we had just witnessed. His response was to the effect that we should "just wait and see what happens next."

It is not unusual for men to seek physical distance from situations they aren't sure how they're going to handle until they decide how they're going to handle them.

I responded that, although I was sensitive to his need to think this through alone, I needed to clear my mind before I could go on to other things. Suggesting he serve as a sounding board, I proceeded to verbally sort the matter out. I sensed that he was through listening long before I was through discussing, but I gave him an "A for effort" and thanked him for communicating. (To many men, this *is* communicating.) And we both moved happily on to the next challenge of the day.

Several things happened in that exchange that are fairly typical in male-female relationships. First, it is not unusual for men to seek physical distance from situations they aren't sure how they're going to handle until they decide how they're going to handle them, whether personal conflict, problems with children, or money or job issues. I refer to this place of retreat as a "hideaway." There are all kinds of hideaways: books are hideaways, television is a hideaway, the workbench in the garage is a hideaway. I'm sure you could identify many more.

Try to see these "hideaways" for what they are and allow them to be positive retreats, as appropriate. However, don't let them be the easy outs for your husband to avoid communication that is important to your relationship or family.

Men want to be alone at times for a variety of reasons—and seldom are those reasons a rejection of you. Some days are simply bad days—just like yours—but they don't want to talk about that or sort it out. Sometimes they're blue, sometimes they're tired, and sometimes they just don't want to engage emotionally. Whatever you do or say when he's in the "I want to be alone" mood, he'll think it's designed to make him feel bad. Likely it will elicit a retaliatory response, so just let a mood like this pass—unless it goes on for too long.

Interestingly, there is a caveat to this "being alone" business. Men really do like to be left alone by you—as long as you don't leave the house. You see, to them, your very presence is often all the company they need. Don't feel deserted when they seek their "hideaway" even though you've made a conscious effort to be available. They often don't feel complete without the security and warmth of your presence, though unacknowledged. Without you, it is not a home.

If this bothers you, find an appropriate time to talk it through and express in positive ways your own needs in this regard. He can't meet your needs if he doesn't know them. Be smart enough as a couple not to let either of your feelings be discounted.

Men generally process details about their partners' behavior only when there's a problem that really impacts their life. This means men are generally less critical of their wives, but once they do become critical, they can become totally focused on that and often can't leave a matter alone until they perceive it as fixed.

As to problem solving, women, if your method is by talking things through, help your partner understand and respect this as a valuable and important tool in your relationship. Don't retreat if at first he doesn't see the value of discussion. Reach out and involve him in nonjudgmental ways. It is important that you say what you have to say—but not everything you have to say.

Men want to be told that they've achieved the "hard" thing, or moved an issue forward. They want you to ask them direct questions and really listen to their answers before formulating your response.

Whether you're in a marriage partnership, a business partnership, or a church partnership, it often works best when dealing with men to end the conversation before you are really ready but after you've had enough dialogue that you know you are both "singing out of the same hymnbook," so to speak. The goal is for each to feel success in the dialogue.

Another tool for successful communication with the men in your life is found in the words you choose. Men relate better to words that sound masculine and logical. (Let me remind you that they start life by trying to make logical sense of the mobile over their crib.) Someone has joked that the words that will get the greatest attention from a man are: "Let me get you your power drill," followed by "You're so strong."

Now, I don't know if that is true, but I do know that when you use words such as "your point is irrefutable" or "you've brought such logic to the discussion," the door is opened for further dialogue.

Men want to be told that they've achieved the "hard" thing, or moved an issue forward. They want you to ask them direct questions and really listen to their answers before formulating your response. And they will hear you better if you are direct in your answer—they're not much for the diplomatic turn and the long buildup. Women, you're the experts with words; pick the ones that will do the job.

The secret for successful relationships with the men in your life is the same as it is for any other relationship, and it has to do with knowing and placing value on who they are specifically, not generally. It's about letting the man you love know of his value in your eyes. It's about letting him know he is the right man for you by articulating daily at least one specific reason why he is that man. You are the fair damsel he wants to impress. You are the reason he will do almost anything to be a hero. You are why he signed on to be provider, protector, lover, consort, and companion.

CHAPTER 4

THREE THINGS WOMEN WISH MEN UNDERSTOOD ABOUT THEM

J ust as men came to earth knowing they were to be heroes, there are few little girls who do not automatically know that a tiara is their right and the wand an extension of their arm, that somehow they are majestic and wonderful, intended to awaken, inform, organize, and civilize all around them.

Anyone who has spent any time with little girls understands quickly that their desire is not to wait passively to be saved, as the fairy tales portray, but rather to set the stage, direct all the players, and be the star of the production.

Little girls know instinctively that their Creator intended them to be and to act as queens—real queens. A girl seems to understand from the time she holds her first doll and sets up housekeeping with her first tea set that she, along with a partner, is to establish her own kingdom over which she and her king will rule and reign.

Little girls are amazingly bright; they learn quickly and feel deeply. They build make-believe medical centers and enlist the boys as the walking wounded; they organize food to take to the homeless shelter and set up lemonade stands to raise money for the starving children of Africa.

I remember when our own little girl had just passed her fourth birthday. Night was falling; the lights of the city were coming on one by one. As darkness descended, they sparkled like jewels. After a long time of watching the lights, this little girl turned to her father and said: "Daddy, I'll give all my jewels to the poor if I can just have a kitty to care for."

Though they twirl and swish and dress up and demand that their brothers do the same—which they often reluctantly do—they can change in a minute and kick the ball, run the bases, happily make mud pies, and catch the odd bug. Their interest, however, is generally to save the bug rather than to dissect it.

Previously we discussed Eve's biblical introduction, in the original Hebrew, as one who rescues or saves. The second word used to describe her combines attributes of both majesty and strength. And then God says that she is to be equal with Adam. This gives us such clear insight into what women would like you to know about them, all of which was borne out in my surveys of and conversations with women.

1. Women have an inherent sense of their majesty, their strength, and their equality. Women do not just want but *need* to have real value placed on their strengths, on their missions, and on their "voice." They need to have an opportunity to properly exercise all their gifts. They see husband, home, and family as principal to fulfillment of their missions and core to their happiness.

Smart, observant, and amazingly adaptable, nearly all

women know deep down of their royalty and their responsibility to it. Not long ago I was at a concert with a young mother, joined by her two children and their friend. Following the concert we were taken through a special tunnel on "people movers." The two endearing girls of about nine said they would ride in the seat facing backward, as they needed to greet the others along the way. The young boy of seven helped them up and stood at the ready as protector while the two queens (they made it clear they were queens, not princesses) nodded and waved the "queens' wave" to everyone we passed along the way.

I was speaking of this to a friend who has had a most successful life as a wife and mother. After her children were grown, she had launched a flourishing career. As I related the above experience, she identified with it immediately. With hunger in her voice, she whispered: "And when you're young and no one lets you be the queen, you spend your whole life trying to figure out what you are to be instead."

She then related the trauma she had faced as a lone child being shuffled from divorced parents to grandparents to others. No one ever made her feel like a princess, much less a queen. She tried her best to excel so they would notice how special she was. Their lack of awareness of her "divine within" made even her triumphs hollow—and sixty years later she still felt that deprivation.

Part of majesty is beauty. And women do love to be beautiful, to be told they're beautiful, and to have beautiful things. I'm sure it comes as no surprise that most women have a keen awareness of their appearance, clothes, and surroundings. Most women want to shop for lovely things, they want to own good-looking things, and they want to be told that what they're wearing is amazing, or that you like their shoes, or that the color of their dress makes their eyes incredible.

When a woman asks a man, "Does this look good?" she wants him to tell her that it does—unless it really doesn't. This is not a time for unvarnished analysis. To be seen as beautiful in every aspect, to be told she is beautiful in every respect (both body and spirit), is as important to a woman as it is to a man to be told he is manly and important and a hero. That is why women will worry and fret and fuss and take exercise and personal growth classes and get facials and buy skin-care products and ask you if they're getting fat or if they look as good as the other women at the party. Men, surely you're smart enough to know the correct answers to those two questions, but in case you're struggling, the answer to the first question is "no," the second, "yes." Always.

To be seen as beautiful in every aspect, to be told she is beautiful in every respect (both body and spirit), is as important to a woman as it is to a man to be told he is manly and important and a hero.

Most men see their home as their castle and would like it to be practical and easy to fortify, with a minimum of frills. If it were possible a man would have a roaring open fire, the hounds at his feet, his spurs on the wall, and his sword at the door. Most women see their home as their palace, their sovereign kingdom, and they feel a deep need to make that home a haven, to embellish and arrange and fix. They need warmth and safety, order and control, things picked up, and some possessions that are not necessarily practical. They need you to understand, embrace, and accept these needs.

Women, be sure your man has his perfect chair, his "hideaway," his desk, his television, and his tools, and likely he'll support and may even help you in creating and fixing and decorating your "palace." It will help if you can make his logical brain understand how this benefits everyone and how important it is to you.

Most women see their home as their palace, their sovereign kingdom, and they feel a deep need to make that home a haven, to embellish and arrange and fix.

2. Women have a particular understanding of the importance of relationships and place highest priority on them. They need to connect at a very personal level, especially with their husbands and children. Heavily invested in their emotions, they are deeply affected by memories, by sights and sounds and touch. Men, ignore this at your peril!

Because of the high priority women place on relationships, their radar is always picking up any static that interrupts that essential connectedness. Seldom is everything all right for everyone about them. This makes verbalizing emotions and feelings and happenings as natural—and essential—to them as breathing.

There is a reason women are often found in the kitchen and the family room, and that reason is positive and has less to do with tasks than one would suspect. Here is where the real networking in the family goes on. Here is where a woman can see and feel what's up with her children, with their interactions, their priorities, and their needs. Here is where she can sit at the table with her husband over a snack and just talk about things. Here is where she can see what's being watched on TV or what's happening with the computer, without being the policeman. And she can do her own work at the same time. This companionable being together, without necessarily all doing the same thing, brings security and comfort to everyone gathered around, although it probably will never be verbalized.

Women hate being objectified, or having you objectify other women, or being subjected to games of objectifying one-upsmanship. Men, don't play those games even in times of male bonding; they corrode the soul.

For a woman, feelings of worth and particularly of love are imprinted by words, sights, sounds, and smells. That's why sunsets and walks and favorite songs are so important to them. That's why the linens need to be nice and the scented candles lit. That's why they ask, "What do you think we'll be doing a year from now?" or "Do you remember what we were doing a year ago?" and why words and acts of love are paramount.

One brilliant young mother wrote: "You must *show* a woman she is loved by making her a top priority." Then, using words with which men can identify, she continued: "As an economist or mathematician would put it: words are a necessary condition, but not a sufficient condition to making a woman feel loved." Another wrote: "It's not enough to tell a woman you love her, you need to tell her *why* you love her." Yet another said, "A woman can never hear 'I love you' too much.

If you're feeling it, *say* it—and when accompanied by a hug or kiss or some sort of touch, it just gets sweeter."

Women think much more about what a man needs than men do about a woman's needs. And they notice much more when something good is done for them and remember much longer when something is neglected—or something bad is done. This is because a woman's brain calendars and prioritizes events based on the emotions evoked by that event. One of women's innate thought processes is a tendency to habitually observe and process data about how their partners behave. This isn't something they do once in a while; this process continues virtually all the time.

> *Women think much more about what a man needs than men do about a woman's needs. And they notice much more when something good is done for them and remember much longer when something is neglected.*

That's why setting a weekly date night and actually sharing in the planning of something to do for that weekly date night is huge. That's why remembering birthdays and anniversaries matters to them—and if you don't remember, they won't soon forget that. That's why they remember that you did something really bad six years ago on September 17th. Women should try to tame this "six years remembering" brain track—it's not going to bring happiness to either of you—but the rest is something men need to keep in mind.

3. Women have a deep knowledge of spiritual things and an extraordinary sense of loyalty. They are uniquely connected to the promptings of the Spirit, to the heavens, to God's voice. They "get it."

This makes most women prescient, perceptive, discerning, and intuitive; almost any scientific study will attest to this. It is in their brain structure, their DNA, their nature—their souls. Why are we surprised? Eve's contract to become the mother of all living was with God. Women similarly sense their relationship and connection with God at a very personal level.

At a recent general conference, Elder D. Todd Christofferson spoke of his travels in many countries and commented: "I have been impressed with the faith and capacity of our women, including some of the very young. So many of them possess a remarkable faith and goodness. They know the scriptures. They are poised and confident. I ask myself, Do we have men to match these women?" ("Let Us Be Men," 47).

DISCUSSION BREAK

Ladies, it's your turn to get out your list of the three things you wish your husband understood about you and discuss them. Men, please listen very carefully and make notes if necessary.

CHAPTER 5

ADDED INSIGHTS

⁓

We've discussed God's plan that men and women are to be equal, and should be equally honored and valued. President James E. Faust reminded us: "Nowhere does the doctrine of this Church declare that men are superior to women" ("Highest Place of Honor," 36). What, then, is it that women want? Once again, there are three major areas of concern:

1. Women want an adult partnership, not a controlling relationship. What most women are seeking in the notion of equality is not *sameness*. Rather, they ask that equal value and weight be placed on their contributions, their intellect, their choices, their voices, their concerns for those in their caring network.

Men, you need to guard against letting your natures as hero-warriors extend to your becoming overly controlling. Your desire to protect can become a need to subordinate, and your desire to provide can call forth, even subconsciously, a feeling of being entitled to govern and to turn your loved ones into your subjects. Thus we see noble incentives used to corrupt and suborn God's plans and purposes.

Recently Dr. Phil McGraw, of the *Dr. Phil* television show, was trying to help a couple who were plagued by what the husband saw as his right to control his wife. It started with his requiring her to ask him for every penny she spent, although he said she could have what she asked for if it wasn't too much. Who would decide what was "too much"? He would.

This meant that he could control all personal items she bought, when the couple came and went, when and where they would vacation, when the children could get anything new. Doctor Phil spent the entire show exploring why this was wrong, interviewing other couples with the same problem, and reinforcing the harm in it. Near the end of the program, feeling sure that the husband had learned the intended positive relationship lessons, Dr. Phil asked if he could support his wife in something she wished to undertake. The husband's reply: "Well, I guess I can *let* her do that." The good doctor nearly went into orbit as he loudly asserted that marriage is about partnership, not about "letting." This brought to my mind all the women who had come to me over the years with similar problems.

One particular young friend was concerned that her husband might not "let" her take some art classes she wanted so desperately. She had been a good artist and thought that this would not only advance her talents but provide needed recreation away from the pressures of a very busy life as a mother of three. But then she said: "He never lets me do anything. He wants to make every decision about everything."

I find that this word *let* crops up in the dialogue with many frustrated and unhappy women who are involved in ongoing relationships. *Let* is not a term proper for a mature relationship. It indicates that someone is in a superior position to allow or give permission to one who should be treated as a partner—an equal. It has no place in godlike partnerships.

However, dear women, do not confuse *your* need to have a sense of control with being a controlling woman. That is a trait that sends men running. You know those women well: They're the ones who always have to do things their way, have the last word, won't let others into their kitchens unless everything is done exactly as they have deigned, won't allow a pillow or a hair to be out of place, won't give their children space to breathe, won't allow their husband a half hour to read the paper because of their to-do list for him, always know how to get it done and want it done their way. They too need to let go of the word *let*.

It's probably wise to agree with your husband that you'll approach all differences in three ways: his way, your way, and another way. Talk about it—chances are, you'll figure something out.

2. Women's lives are expressed in words; they need to be talked with and listened to. "Women use 20,000 words a day, men only 7,000," heralds the *Boston Globe*. The writer of this article noted that "a bit of Googling" easily turns up at least nine different versions of this claim, ranging from 50,000 words for women versus 25,000 for men down to 5,000 versus 2,500 words respectively. Conversely, a recent report of audio clips from university students showed that at that age both sexes use about the same number of words (see Liberman, "The Female Brain"; Allday, "Men Gab Just As Much").

In truth, the actual number of words used by men versus women doesn't really matter. Most of us in adult relationships recognize that there is a disparity, and that disparity makes true communicating of ideas and needs difficult.

Recent brain imaging studies also show that more of a woman's brain is involved in language skills than a man's, and more of her brain time is spent reading the emotions and needs of others and tying those emotions and needs to expressed language. That helps explain why women feel an urgency to communicate, whereas men—not so much. It also points to the fact that in order to make this whole communication thing work, women will want to do some real conversational and emotional editing, and men will need to learn to do a lot more tuned-in listening and a bit more conversational expanding.

Men, let me share a little secret with you: Your words—and your approval, expressed in those words—are exhilarating to the woman in your life! You can make her feel like a queen with just a few of the right words. And because her world revolves around language and feelings, lots of "I understand what you're feeling," and "Would you like to talk?" will do wonders for your togetherness.

You don't even have to talk much, just be present and ask the odd question at an appropriate pause. But do listen to what your wife or girlfriend is saying. To be deeply, sincerely listened to is one of the things women want most—and one of the things many feel a lack of in their relationships. That capacity to listen was also one of the things the women I surveyed felt made men "really desirable."

At the end of the day my husband will often come to me and say, "I've used up all my words for the day." (You can see from this that we've had the "word count" discussions.) By that, he generally means, "The good sports programs are coming on and I'd like it if I wasn't interrupted." If I want to talk, or have something light on my mind, I'll say: "Sorry, dear, I haven't used all mine. But all you need to do is listen." Then I keep it short and fun. I try not to bring up the problems of the day at this time, just stuff I want to share. We both end the day happy.

My son and his wife have a good policy in their home: They won't discuss anything troublesome or heavy after eight in the evening. This policy came about because she would often tell him of her challenges right at the end of the day, and rather than just listen, he would try to solve them (we talked about this earlier). That left her frustrated and him with his protector juices roiling, primed to slay dragons she didn't want or need him to slay.

Though most women have this desire to be verbally connected, it can be taken to the extreme. We all know needy women who can find no happiness in themselves or in their lives, so they cling to others in hopes of filling the void. They call their children several times a day, when a call every day to an adult child is probably too much. They interrupt their friends' or spouses' days too often, making them feel both frustrated and uneasily guilty. A married woman with this problem can demand too much from her husband in the way of support and time and energy, leaving no time or room for him to regenerate and just "be."

On the other side of the spectrum, some women will suffer abuse in the name of connectedness rather than take steps to get away from the abuser. Some women give themselves over to untrustworthy men or don't ask for what they need from and deserve in a relationship lest that connectedness disappear. And there are far too many men who will take advantage of this.

Be alert to the possibility of both extremes in your relationship. Neither is a way to happiness. But true, healthy connectedness is lifeblood to a woman.

We've talked about the five senses, which are so keen in women. Smell is second in imprint only to sight. Therefore looking and smelling good, along with sharing flowers and little surprises and good music and laughter, will make her think you're very, very "hot"—and will go a long way toward keeping the romance alive. If you're married, so will taking out the garbage, picking up your socks, changing diapers, and vacuuming.

A brilliant young mother, musician, and scholar wrote: "I wish men knew how much women appreciate small acts of kindness—making the bed, sharing work experiences, getting up early with the kids, a note now and then. I think that men feel they always need to do big things, like lead the family, buy diamonds, plan big trips. But really women just need day-to-day thoughtfulness and inclusion in men's lives."

A woman needs to feel confident in seeking closeness through both touch and conversation. To be able to express one's thoughts, feelings, hopes, and dreams is a higher form of development that women tend to grasp more easily than men do. Some women expressed this caution: "When a woman wants to talk and needs comforting, she most often just wants to be held and cherished for who she is, not for what she can give. Save the lovemaking overtures for another time."

Men expect to be thanked for everything they've done around the house, even though it may be their agreed-upon assignment. Women don't expect to be thanked for everything, but they'd like to be thanked for *something*. Men, the more you notice and thank, the more hugs and kisses you'll get and the more likely you are to be seen as the hero.

3. Women's deep prescience and spirituality are often frightening to men.

Women are deeply attuned to the needs of their families. This attunement and prescience and depth of spirituality explains why a man honoring his priesthood is important to women, why a wife, mother, or woman worries when the man she loves becomes complacent in the gospel, why women would really like the boys and men in their lives to attend all their meetings and to stay awake during sacrament meetings. They know who men are, how important their continuing spiritual growth is, and how much men need to stay in tune spiritually so that they can exercise the priesthood power upon which both men and women are so dependent.

This heightened awareness is often tied to a woman's sense that she must get her family back safely to their heavenly home. One woman wrote: "I think men would be humbled and touched if they could see into a woman's heart and see how much she wants to be a good mother and have her family return to Heavenly Father. I wish men knew how desperately women want our families to succeed and be happy."

Trust women's feelings, their intuition, and their deep

spiritual gifts. Listen to the promptings of the woman in your life. She may well be in touch at a different level with the Holy Ghost. And she is likely more in tune with the needs and feelings of her family members.

As noted, men would much rather deal with the hard, cold facts of right and wrong, black and white, good and evil. Because of traits that are commonly though certainly not exclusively female, women tend to see both sides of things, and therefore they lean to mercy in most matters (see Baron-Cohen, "They Just Can't Help It").

Perhaps this helps us understand why the scales of justice are held by a woman. Perhaps it explains why mercy, when spoken of in the Bible, is given feminine gender. A story is told of the Algonquin tribes of the Northeast, after whose government some say our founding fathers patterned ours. It seems they felt that if justice was to be properly dispensed it had to have an element of mercy in it. Therefore, their supreme court was made up entirely of women.

While women are discerning, brilliant, and intuitive, they also are often intensely loyal, a loyalty that can expand beyond that which will serve their best interests. This deep loyalty applies not just to

Trust women's feelings, their intuition, and their deep spiritual gifts. Listen to the promptings of the woman in your life. She may well be in touch at a different level with the Holy Ghost. And she is likely more in tune with the needs and feelings of her family members.

personal relationships, but often to business and social relationships.

Women want to be forgiving and therefore often forgive the unforgivable. Their sense of loyalty can thus get them in trouble. It is innate in their nature to trust their protector to protect, their lover to love, and their spiritual leader to be spiritual. They will stay in a bad relationship, support an errant cause, and stand by a negative friend far longer than may be good for them or for those around them. Weak men trade on this.

It is important for men to understand that women are hardwired to connect at all levels with the family of humankind. Men need to recognize the importance of women's life-giving and lifesaving roles. It is useful for men to know that women take seriously their spiritual assignments to bring compassion, mercy, order, and civility to their world. It is *imperative* for men to recognize that women have an innate sense of their own worth and majesty, and that they, along with their vital contributions, need to be properly recognized and significantly valued.

We've just scratched the surface of male-female interactions and only begun to understand the importance for the here and now—and for the eternities—of getting our relationships right. We'll look at these matters in greater detail in Section III of this book.

For now, delight in who you are individually—and in who you are and can be together.

SECTION II

OF VISION AND LOVE

～

Your vision will become clear
only when you look into your heart. . . .
He who looks outside, dreams.
He who looks inside, awakens.

—CARL JUNG

CHAPTER 6

WHAT I LEARNED ABOUT LOVE FROM *THE LITTLE PRINCE*

One of my favorite books is a thin volume written to children and perceptive adults entitled *The Little Prince.* In an insightful and charming way, author Antoine de Saint-Exupéry explores all sorts of relationships through the eyes of a "little prince" who has arrived on a new and unfamiliar planet.

At one point the little prince desires to befriend a fox, but it is difficult because they have nothing in common. The fox tells the little prince that if he will be very patient, they will learn from each other to place value on those things that now have no worth to them. The fox relates that he does not eat bread—therefore the wheat fields have no meaning to him. But if they become friends, the wheat, which is golden, will remind him of the color of the little prince's hair, and he will then love the sound of the wind in the wheat as it blows the heads to and fro. From this kind of interaction, they will learn how to build love.

Yes, love is a building process, and although love feels different to different people, nearly everyone who loves goes through three distinct stages. Those of us who have lived through these stages understand them well, but it's hard for those who are in the middle of one stage or another to believe that things will ever feel different. Being aware of the stages may be helpful when things do seem to change, especially in demonstrating that altered love is not lesser love.

Stage 1: Newly in Love

Falling in love feels so intensely good and can occur so quickly that those involved can sometimes barely keep their footing. That's why it's called "falling." Other phrases people in this phase commonly use to describe it are: "I was swept off my feet," "It left my head spinning," and "I've lost my balance." What occurs actually causes chemical changes in your body that can do all of the above. That's why some people actually become addicted to the falling-in-love part of a relationship but can't quite carry through with the staying-in-love stage.

Why does this happen? It's because of the endorphins that the falling stage releases in the brain. These endorphins cause that disquieting yet wonderful feeling of heady anticipation; they cause the butterflies in the stomach, the heart that races, and the feelings of mad eagerness to be together. There is a "newly in love" molecule racing madly through your entire body.

Scientists have now isolated that molecule and given it the very unromantic name of "nerve growth factor," or NGF (see

"Blame the 'Love Molecule'"). These Italian scientists found far higher levels of NGF in the blood of people who had recently fallen madly in love than in that of control groups of singles and people in long-term relationships.

However, this new love with all its powerful passions has a shelf life of approximately one year. Perhaps such strong emotions burn too hot for the heart and body to bear over the long run. After a year with the same lover, the quantity of the "love molecule" in the experimental subjects' blood had fallen to the same level as that of the other groups.

Stage 2: Growing in Love

Love is intended to grow and mature. After the "newly in love" phase has passed, you are emotionally and physically designed to move to the next stage. This is the settling-in part. You adore each other, you laugh at each other's jokes, you see the future as open to all kinds of possibilities, and you're excited about the promise: the first real home, the last college degree, the new career, the waiting children. Nonetheless, the little irritations begin to set in. Before long, you've begun trying to make your partner over to be more like you. This desire to "redesign" happens to just about every couple.

Why is this? Scientists tell us that nature causes us to unconsciously seek a mate who is opposite ourselves. Our instincts lead us to desire that which will make us complete— whole. We are naturally attracted to that one, opposite ourselves, who will bring an entire new set of actions, ideas, powers, and talents to the table, thus fortifying us for the long journey ahead and assuring continued strengthening of the gene pool.

And so in our search for a mate we see differences as intriguing. Those differences open entire new vistas of thought and action. They seem so fresh and desirable and—well—different.

However, not long after marriage, those traits, actions, and attitudes that were so compellingly wonderful because of their novelty can become a bit irksome. At least one in the partnership generally begins wondering, "Why can't he (or she) be more like me?" Soon they're engaged in trying to make small changes in each other, then larger ones.

Unless someone in the relationship finally figures out how wrong it is for them to try to turn each other into carbon copies of themselves, far too many people spend a good portion of their lives trying to make their partners over in their own images. That doesn't make any sense. You already have your own strengths—strengths that will be multiplied if you see your partner's differences as assets and add them to the mix. The miracle in any marriage is not how alike two people are but how they have been able to value, accept, and accommodate their differences.

Like the little prince, you can identify, embrace, and learn to place value on your differences. Accept the fact that most couples have a different vision about almost everything—except, hopefully, the "biggies," which we will discuss later.

Stage 3: A Love to Die For, Worthy of Living For

You've probably heard of the "seven-year itch," a phrase used to typify the time spent in stage 2 negotiating the differences in a marriage. After safely passing through that stage, couples generally reach the third stage of love. We can learn a lot about this phase from *The Little Prince.* The prince has come to deeply love a single rose. He talks about how many other roses there are, and how most passersby would say they all looked alike. Addressing a large field of roses, he explains how he can tell the difference:

"My rose, all on her own, is more important than all of you together since she's the one I've watered. Since she's the one I sheltered behind a screen. Since she's the one for whom I killed the caterpillars (except the two or three for butterflies). Since she's the one I listened to when she complained, or when she boasted, or even sometimes when she said nothing at all" (Saint-Exupéry, *Little Prince,* 63).

The great lesson is that through loving and serving one another, we build a forever love. Here's the really good part about this kind of love: Though your commitment may be tested over and over, if you've done the work, listened to each other, and included God as your partner, you know you'll make it. You'll have forged a glorious diamond from the white heat of the newly-in-love phase and the pressures of the growing-in-love stage.

Learning the Language of Your Love

Not only does love have its own molecule and its own stages—it also has its own language. We've talked of how words don't mean the same thing to any two people. Therefore, for your marriage to thrive, the two of you together will wish to identify the "language"—that is, the sights, sounds, and smells—of your own unique world. You need to establish your own "rites."

The Little Prince teaches us about this also. The fox, in trying to help the prince understand what a deep friendship means, tells the prince that it would be good if he could come every day at about the same time. "For instance, if you come at four in the afternoon, I'll begin to be happy by three. . . . By four I'll be all excited and worried; I'll discover what it costs to be happy! But if you come at any old time, I'll never know when I should prepare my heart. . . . There must be rites."

The little prince has never heard the word *rites* before and he asks what it means. "It's the fact that one day is different from the other days, one hour from the other hours," the fox tells him. "My hunters, for example, have a rite. They dance with the village girls on Thursdays. So, Thursday's a wonderful day; I can take a stroll all the way to the vineyards" (Saint-Exupéry, *Little Prince,* 61). It is important to establish "rites" unique to your love so that anticipation keeps that love alive.

We've mentioned the emotional power of the sense of smell. This principle was brought home to me by a television movie, based on a true story, about a man who was still trying to find his footing a full two years after his wife's death. He related to a friend that the thing he could never forget was her smell on the pillow. He thought it was her perfume, and spent hours at perfume counters trying to find the scent. Then one day, as another woman passed him, that smell wafted through the air. He followed the woman for blocks and finally realized it was her hair that smelled good. It was the scent of the shampoo left by his beloved's hair on the pillow that he longed to know once again. Such a simple thing—but part of the language of love.

It took me years to figure out that having lots of different perfumes may have pleased me and my moods, but there was only one perfume that elicited notice and attention from my husband. From that time on, that has been the only perfume I wear when I'm near him.

Connection is also about sounds. One husband spoke of the security he felt when he came into his home and heard his wife's music playing in the background. That meant she was home and all was well. He loved coming home to that familiar sound and hated coming home to silence. And a wife told me how her whole body smiled when she heard her husband whistle. It meant he was near and he was happy.

My husband and I have many memories of times when we've entered a square or a restaurant or a park and heard just the right music playing. Immediately we're flooded with joy and aliveness; we clasp hands and smile and know we're so lucky to be where we are and to be together. We have made it a point, when traveling, to always find at least one such place we can frequent while there. For us, this is planting one more "memory rose."

Sight is huge in relationships. A husband told me his heart jumps when he sees someone with dark hair wearing anything red. Why? Because his lovely, dark-haired wife wore red a lot, and that color had come to mean her presence. I asked her about this, and she said, "I wear red because he seems to love it so." Without knowing it, each had acceded to the other, and together they had created their own "sight language."

Pay close attention to those things that make up the language of your partnership, those things you love together, . . . that make your hearts jump, or sing, or beat a bit faster.

You are creating your own sovereign kingdom, a world unique unto yourselves. Pay close attention to those things that make up the language of your partnership, those things you love together, those things your husband or wife loves uniquely, those things that make your hearts jump, or sing, or beat a bit faster, things that make you laugh or that stir your soul. Make them an absolute and positive part of the "rites" of your shared world. *There have to be rites!*

CHAPTER 7

CLUES TO LOVE'S VISION

———

Vision is an interesting word, isn't it? In a secular sense, *vision* often refers to the power of anticipating what might happen in the future, particularly as it relates to business trends. In a religious sense, the word *vision* is about revelations; it implies seeing beyond the obvious, looking through the lens of the Spirit to perceive lasting truths. In either sense, people who "catch the vision" are brought to a deeper feeling of purpose and a greater awareness of their true selves. They awaken more fully to the mission ahead.

Eve's last beautiful gesture, after she had awakened to the truths of their mission and journey together, was to reach her hand out to her beloved Adam and ask him to join her. Her declarations of love and intent were clear and purposeful: Together, they would keep *all* of Father's commands.

In humility Adam and Eve set off into the unknown, to deal with whatever life placed in their path, to solve all problems and share all joys. They knew they were to stay together, have a family, and grow in the ordinances, in love, in learning, and in oneness until they could return, hand in hand, to dwell again with their Father. They embraced their partnership not just as a committed union but as a covenant union.

This full commitment to the marriage covenant is so central to our mission that a singular and prophetic *Proclamation to the World* was issued regarding the centrality of marriage and the family to the gospel plan. Its first sentence reads: "We, the First Presidency and the Council of the Twelve Apostles of The Church of Jesus Christ of Latter-day Saints, solemnly proclaim that marriage between a man and a woman is ordained of God and that the family is central to the Creator's plan for the eternal destiny of His children."

The importance of the marriage covenant is underlined by these words of Elder L. Tom Perry: "The union between husband and wife is not something to be trifled with. The marriage covenant is essential for the Lord to accomplish His divine purposes. Consistently the Lord has declared that His divine laws were instituted to safeguard and protect the holy union between husband and wife" ("An Elect Lady," 72).

And don't think for a moment that God is the only one interested in this covenant venture! Satan's head must twirl like a pinwheel in a high wind each time he senses a covenant marriage relationship being formed. He and his minions will seek every opportunity to short-circuit that relationship at any of its many stages.

Many young couples—as well as several older ones—have told me that though they have glimmers of understanding as to their partnership role, they still aren't confident that they have "caught the vision." In fact, some have said they quite often feel clueless as they seek to find a common cause in this, the most important of all life's roles.

That should not be the case. There are clues—and they're not from the board game where it's about Colonel Mustard with the candlestick in the library. These are real clues, and they come directly from God. Following are three such clues to help you understand and create a vision for your own relationships.

Clue #1: Love's Partnership Is about the Vision

Just as Adam and Eve left their garden home for a "cold-water flat" in an unfamiliar and puzzling world, such it seems is the pattern for all who enter marriage. After the vows are spoken, you've both entered uncharted territory, for though there have been millions of marriages,

After the vows are spoken, you've both entered uncharted territory, for though there have been millions of marriages, none have been or ever will be just like yours.

none have been or ever will be just like yours. There is a whole new world out there just waiting for you as a couple to identify, master, and conquer it. That's one of the many things that make marriage so exciting, so challenging, and so filled with promise.

Not long after entering this new world, however, you'll discover a foreign language being spoken—and it's not outside your home, it's inside it. You'll perceive that words don't always mean the same thing to your partner that they do to you. You may have few common life experiences. Chances are, you haven't articulated clearly your vision of what marriage would do or be or bring to you.

A presidential power broker and I were exploring the reasons some presidents were great and others mediocre. The identifying word this brilliant technician kept using was *vision.* He described one president's success: "He had a vision and he was committed to that vision." Of another president, he said, "He had magnetism, but he couldn't make important things happen because he had no vision." Of yet another, he said, "He had a vision but he didn't have the courage to fight for it when everything seemed to be going against it."

From these examples I recognized the truth in the admonition from Proverbs: "Where there is no vision, the people perish" (Proverbs 29:18). I also grasped that it is not enough to just have a vision—we must have an absolute commitment to that vision. That commitment must be followed by the boldness to live the vision regardless of the distractions. In the words of Antoine de Saint-Exupéry, "Love does not consist in gazing at each other but in looking together in the same direction."

It follows, then, that the foundation of a great presidency, a great partnership, or a great covenant marriage is based on shared dreams, understood mental images, and joint goals. Add to this a commitment to expend the energy, time, and resources to give that vision life, and amazing things will happen!

Clue #2: Images Shape Our Reality, Our Perception, Our Vision

Pierce and I were at a workshop some years ago where the presenter asked each of us, as couples, to look at the same picture and without discussion make separate lists of what we saw. As the lists were revealed, we discovered that we had focused on entirely different elements within the same picture. From our written lists, it appeared we had not even been looking at the same print. This was true of every couple in the room. Not one couple shared a common vision of what they were looking at together in real time and in living color.

Try this exercise with your spouse, or with the one you're thinking of committing to. Both what you see and what you don't see will give you important insight about the lenses through which you each perceive the world.

Our mental images and perceptions of visual images differ depending on our life experiences, examples, expectations, and gender. And our responses to these images shape our reality, and thus our actions and reactions. The point of this exercise is not for the two of you to see the same thing; it's about understanding that you likely *won't* see the same thing in most situations.

As you become more fully attuned to this concept, you will recognize that, as a couple, you need to explore your individual realities together and talk them through. Until you do so, you're not likely to find comfortable common language—common ground—common cause.

A woman in her late twenties expressed to me that her love was at low ebb. Her words were: "My marriage is simply not turning out the way I planned or dreamed." She went on to explain that the picture she had in her mind for a good marriage was patterned after the family she had been raised in, with a few added embellishments of her own. She hadn't anticipated so many compromises—compromises that became less palatable with each passing year.

"It's not what I wanted; it's not what I envision a good marriage to be," she plaintively reported. This mental image, the vision, she had created of what her husband and marriage would be like was inconsistent with the reality now before her—which, incidentally, didn't sound all that bad, just inconsistent with her vision. Possibly what was happening was inconsistent with her husband's vision of marriage as well.

Many couples struggle with unrealistic expectations as to what their marriage should deliver in terms of emotional support, homes, cars, lifestyle, "keeping up appearances," and so on.

Most couples have a different vision of what a day, a vacation, or even just an evening spent together will look like. One says, "It's Saturday, how about slipping out for lunch and a movie?" The mental picture in the person's mind is a long-awaited movie about feelings, preceded by a lovely, sit-down lunch at a favorite Italian cafe. The other visualizes grabbing a quick sandwich at the snack bar and slipping into whatever movie fits in the time schedule and looks most attention-grabbing. I'll let you guess which gender has which picture in mind. If words for a simple afternoon out create different visions, can you begin to imagine what differences in vision are conjured up relating to the "biggies" of your life, and therefore why important needs can often go unmet?

Besides unmet needs, many couples struggle with unrealistic expectations as to what their marriage should deliver in terms of emotional support, homes, cars, lifestyle, "keeping up appearances," and so on. More often than not, both heads of this monster—unmet needs and unrealistic expectations—are at work devouring a couple's present and future happiness.

Clue #3: It's Important—and Possible—to Identify the Roots of Your Vision Problems

Wouldn't you believe that two adult people in a marriage partnership would be smart enough to find ways to accommodate their essential needs? Does it amaze you that so many are unable to find common ground for their expectations so that they can begin to feel some happiness?

Where do unrealistic expectations begin? More often than not, our "vision seeds" are planted long before marriage as we form a clear and detailed mental image of the person we will wed. Generally this is a positive image, and we form it with the best of intentions, based on values, desires, and life experiences.

For example, a young woman says to a young man, "I want to marry a man just like my father." The young man says, "I can be that person." But the young woman's picture of what her father did and said, how he acted around the house, how he provided for the family, the way he honored the Sabbath or exercised his priesthood, is likely entirely different from the image the young man conjures up in his mind, for his pictures are based on his own experiences.

The young man says, "I want a wife who is beautiful and will be a true companion to me." She says, "I can do that." What he means is: "I want to hike and camp and really rough it. I want to go to action movies and spend Monday nights, after a much-abbreviated family home evening, watching the football games. And no matter how many children we have, I want you to always look like the girl of my dreams."

What she means is: "We'll do everything together. We'll talk and share and plan and decorate and have candlelight dinners and long walks in the sunset and follow the Church's programs exactly, and I'll always be beautiful to you."

They each create their own mental pictures to go with the words that have been said. It never even occurrs to either that there might be a difference in what mental pictures those words bring to their partner. Thus unrealistic expectations are born even when a couple seems at first to be in agreement.

As a youth or a young adult, did you ever get together with friends or sit in a class and record a long list of qualities you were searching for in a mate? These lists keep lots of people from marrying—or, if they do marry, and the spouse doesn't live up to the list, there's a whole lot of disappointment and discontent.

I remember, as a young girl, making such lists. In fact, my girlfriends and I loved these lists. We felt so hopeful and in many ways smugly sure and safe. We would settle for nothing less, and if the man we married didn't continue to exhibit all of these traits, we would insist that he become that person. The fact that such a man probably did not exist did not for one moment cross our minds. Our leaders applauded us for our ability to identify such highly desirable and laudable traits, and advised us to keep our goals high.

I do not wish to negate the sincerity of heart or the noble intent with which these suggestions were advanced. Of course, we should help each other reach for the stars, set lofty goals, and above all keep our standards high. If we don't have the dream, we may never reach for the best within ourselves. However, somewhere in the back of many a young bride's mind is a picture of herself as a failure because her mate doesn't exhibit all of the traits on the list. Such a picture can only lead to unhappiness. President Gordon B. Hinckley, speaking at a general Relief Society meeting, cautioned the sisters: "Aim high, but do not aim so high that you totally miss the target" ("To the Women of the Church," 114).

By the way, girls are not the only ones who make these lists. I recently spent an evening with a small group of extraordinary single men in their mid-twenties. As we were discussing relationships, I asked them what they were looking for in a partner. They found delight in topping each other with their descriptions of "must haves." In no time at all their list of "won't marry without" reached twenty items.

I said I could understand why they were not yet married: They had just described an illusion. What they were looking for seemed to be an unlikely combination of Keira Knightley and Mother Teresa.

> *"Aim high, but do not aim so high that you totally miss the target."*
>
> *(Gordon B. Hinckley)*

I do feel these "won't settle for less" lists have done marriage and its participants an enormous injustice. If you want, first, to find someone to marry, and second, to keep that marriage alive, you have to confine your dreams to that which is realistic and possible. Throw out the lists and learn instead to articulate the vision.

CHAPTER 8

ESTABLISHING A
SOVEREIGN KINGDOM

—〰—

One of the earliest biblical admonitions regarding relationships says: "Therefore shall a man leave his father and his mother, and shall cleave unto his wife: and they shall be one flesh" (Genesis 2:24). Only within the walls of your own home can you prioritize your needs, assess your strengths and the mutual desires of your hearts, and combine them to build an eternal unit. The plan is that the two of you are to decide together what will work best for your particular partnership. Your marriage will not be like that of your parents, your best friend, or a beloved leader.

God's instructions are unambiguous in this regard— instructions so important that they are among his first recorded utterances to his children on the earth. It is clear that he intends a couple's thoughts and actions to be unified and purposeful. A couple's strength is to be found in their oneness, "cleaving" unto each other, and in their identifying themselves to all others as a whole unit, "and none else" (see D&C 42:22). The husband's work will be the wife's, and the wife's work will be the husband's.

Broader definitions of roles and assignments within a marriage are real and essential. But within that framework, couples need to define, refine, and assign tasks so as to meet the needs they have outlined together and take advantage of the strengths each brings to the table.

Each partner will need to approach this evaluation process with respect for and confidence in the intent and intellect of the other. No success should be claimed unless it is mutually achieved.

Awakening to the Soul, Not Just the Body

A concept often missing from modern thought is that partners are meant to have a noble role in each other's lives. They are meant to help one another find the highest part of their spiritual and personal selves. Partners are to become saviors to one another—leading where needed, following when appropriate, walking side by side when equally strengthened, until together they reach salvation's door.

The plan is that the two of you are to decide together what will work best for your particular partnership. Your marriage will not be like that of your parents, your best friend, or a beloved leader.

Author Thomas Moore addresses this: "At one level marriage is about relationship, but at another it is the creation of a vessel in which soul-making can be accomplished" (Moore, *Soul Mates,* 57). Moore writes of the unusual sensitivity it will take to read one another's souls, the courage it will take to expose one's own soul for the reading, and then the hugely creative but difficult task for two people in a marriage to weave these unfolded souls into a single tapestry of richness and beauty. It's about awakening to one another, just as Adam awakens to Eve.

We find this theme of awakening to one another not only in the scriptures but echoing in ballet, music, and literature. The handsome prince glides across the stage, leans over, and gently kisses the beautiful sleeping princess. She slowly, joyfully, awakens to a world of promise and hope. In opera, it is only after Pamina leads her prince through the ultimate trials of fire and water that he is able to emerge from the darkness and awaken to who he is—and to who she is.

Something wonderful happens in a marriage as souls jointly awaken together to God and to the power of His love, just as God is ever awake to their marriage and the power of their love. So significant is our relationship with God that it caused the Psalmist to exclaim: "What is man, that thou art mindful of him? . . . For thou hast made him a little lower than the angels, and hast crowned him with glory and honour. Thou madest him to have dominion over the works of thy hands; thou hast put all things under his feet" (Psalm 8:4–6).

Awakening to God—Together

A recent study found that couples who incorporate their love of God, their purpose in prayer, their shared commitment to church attendance—that is, their religion—into their daily comings and goings are much less likely to divorce, even when the bad times come, as they surely will. This study also found that those who share a commitment to their religion and practice it together are much more likely to practice marital fidelity and have a stronger commitment to keeping their families intact. It reported less conflict and greater expressed happiness in couples who walked their daily walk together with God (see Weaver, "Shared Religion," 7).

Just going to church together, the study suggested, often helps with those times when it's really difficult to remember all the reasons for your love, your union, your marriage, your covenant. Feeling the spirit in the chapel, hearing the words spoken, and partaking of the sacrament helps each of you focus on what is really important in your relationship.

The study also noted that joint prayer was a great healer. I recall, prior to our marriage, we went to Pierce's beloved former stake president for advice. He said he had just three bits of advice for us: (1) never go to bed angry, (2) never go to bed without praying together, and (3) plant a new "memory rose" every day.

I don't know what I expected to hear, but I was a bit disappointed, as those three things seemed far too simple. Over the years, however, as we have applied those principles to our marriage, I have found them to be profound.

During our early years together there were several times when two o'clock in the morning found us each sitting in a separate room, too upset with one another to reconcile but too committed to that advice to ignore it. Finally, one or the other or both of us would humble ourselves so we could seek a solution to our problem. Then we would pray together and fall exhausted into bed, and in the morning all seemed to be well with us and with the new day. We were now ready to plant our next daily rose—something we have tried to do every day of our married life.

For Latter-day Saints, going to the temple is the ultimate commitment to a love that is forever and always. The sealing ceremony available only in that holy house binds two as one for time and all eternity. It contains amazing promises and provides invaluable information as to who we were before our birth, why we are here, where we are going, and why we are dependent on Jesus the Christ as our Savior.

Because temples are so important to us as spouses, as families, and as individuals, it's hard to understand why any couple would want to begin their journey together anywhere else. Temples are our link between heaven and earth, the only place where we can make the covenants and claim the ordinances that bind us as families and open the way to a place in the celestial kingdom.

President Gordon B. Hinckley speaks of the promises inherent in the divine sealing power: "For the woman who is married in the temple, there is afforded the opportunity for happiness and for security, for time and for all eternity, to a degree to be found in no other type of marriage." He goes on to teach that "the man cannot be exalted without the woman; neither the woman without the man" ("Ten Gifts," 88). And he has recently issued the following challenge to the men of the Church: "I challenge every father and husband to see that he is worthy to take his wife and children to the temple. There is nothing in all this world that will substitute for it. It is the greatest blessing that can come to any couple" ("First Presidency Message," 7).

He encourages us with these words: "I am satisfied that if our people would attend the temple more, there would be less selfishness in their lives. There would be less absence of love in their relationships. There would be more fidelity on the part of husbands and wives. There would be more love and peace and happiness in the homes of our people. There would come into their minds . . . an increased awareness of their relationship to God our Eternal Father." Mothers and fathers are promised that if they will attend the temple regularly, "Your families will draw closer to the Lord; unseen angels will watch over your loved ones when satanic forces tempt them" (Regional Representatives Seminar, April 6, 1984).

The Lord addresses the eternal state of exaltation that can be claimed by those who have been married in his holy temples and have honored their covenants: "Then shall they be gods, because they have no end; therefore shall they be from everlasting to everlasting, because they continue; then shall they be above all, because all things are subject unto them. Then shall they be gods, because they have all power, and the angels are subject unto them" (D&C 132:20).

Healing the Wounds of Our Loved Ones

Most of us forget that by the time we are ready to enter into a marriage we have already lived long enough and been faced with enough of life's challenges, problems, and slights to have been wounded. We all come into marriage bearing scars. As partners, we need to be sensitive to each other's wounds, acknowledging and addressing them lest they become infected and thereby threaten the very relationship itself.

There is an exceptional young man Pierce and I have known since he was a young boy. After his mission he met and fell in love with a beautiful, sensitive, spiritual young woman.

We'll call them Andrew and Melinda. After they married, Andrew pursued a master's degree at a prestigious university. By the time he graduated, two children had joined their family. These two remarkable adults were so involved in their families, their careers, and their church commitments that they had little time to discuss what was happening in each other's personal and emotional lives.

Not long after Andrew was established in his career, a major move was required that took them away from all the usual support systems. After the move, he noticed changes in Melinda but wasn't aware what was happening. One evening he returned home after a grueling day to find the children still in their pajamas, the kitchen floor coated with crushed breakfast cereals, and Melinda hiding in terror behind the couch. She couldn't tell him what was wrong—she only knew she could not face a terrifying "something" that was out there lying in wait for her.

After many visits to doctors and finally to a psychiatrist, the roots of the terror began to be exposed. As a child, this glorious woman had been terrorized by her stepfather. He had repeatedly molested and harmed her. In order to survive, she had buried this trauma deep in the recesses of her mind. It was only after the birth of their children that these experiences began to demand attention and resolution. She had no desire to lend them more credence by giving them voice, so she tried to bury them deeper. But when there was a major break in her support systems, her wounds could no longer be "stuffed" into her mind's recesses, and they came flooding back to haunt her in a crippling way.

They were such terrible wounds, the healing of which would require intense therapy, a love that provided unquestioned and unquestioning safe haven, a trust more powerful than the horrific harm done to one of God's innocents. Was Andrew up to it—was she?

The good news is, yes, they were. Now, some fifteen years later, they have emerged with an amazing and strengthened love and are one another's greatest support. They've done the job of soul building and healing one another's wounds very well. Of course, they would both tell you that it couldn't have happened had they not included God as their partner and turned the ultimate and final healing over to their Lord and Savior, Jesus Christ.

Life has a way of taking such surprising and challenging turns. It is essential that your joint vision be consistent with embracing, sustaining, and supporting one another through *all* of life's challenges, in whatever form they may appear. Your commitment must be to keeping this union for the *full* term, not just the *good* term. It is this sense of "whatever happens, we're together to the end," that builds perfect love.

The Spirit tells us that the power found in love can transform us, change us, refine us, make us reach deeper, and help us achieve things we would never have thought possible. Love is designed to build lives and souls—and to *rebuild* lives and souls that have been broken. Married love is one of the greatest of all earthly powers, a power in which God is uniquely vested. Believe in it. Exercise it. Use it.

DISCUSSION BREAK

Here would be a good time to turn back to the exercise from the Introduction and discuss the three major choices that have shaped your lives individually. You may also wish to answer this question as a couple—talk about three major events that have propelled you together to where you are now. Words and images will begin to take on new meaning once you've done this together.

CHAPTER 9

THE THREE-STONE PRINCIPLE

—⌒—

You now know that for a marriage to endure, the couple must have a clear understanding of what love looks like to each of them, an undying commitment to that love, and a joint vision of how their marriage is to be conducted in all its stages.

Following is an exercise designed to help you be certain that you are sharing and working toward a joint vision. Upon completion of this exercise, you will have identified and articulated a common language and committed yourself with clarity to a common vision. This may take some thought and time and soul searching, but I promise you the results will be worth the effort. If you're wondering if this will really work, read to the end of the chapter before you begin the exercise.

It's important for you to understand that you can make the principles of this exercise work for you no matter where you are in life, whether you are contemplating marriage, already in a marriage of brief or long standing, or in a second marriage or beyond. The steps outlined here will add important and startling new insights and generate amazing dialogue as you and your partner find common cause for the years ahead.

Step One: Define

Start with a blank piece of paper for each of you. Across the top, write the title: "My Vision Statement." Identify and record those three things that are most important to you in a marriage—the three things that you are absolutely unwilling to live in the marriage without. Have your partner do the same. You may have to start with a much longer list and do lots of weeding out. (I have found in looking at final lists that those three items generally are anchored to eternal and family principles.)

On another sheet, write a Defining Statement identifying what those things mean to you in the absolute—no generalization.

On a *third sheet* of paper, outline *why* each of those "can't live withouts" is key to your personal fulfillment and eternal happiness. Thus armed, you are ready to move to the next step.

Step Two: Share

Now, as a couple, bring your lists together for discussion. Put both lists on the table and, item by item, discuss in great detail why each is important to you.

1. Identify from your combined lists three items that are going to be your "together" operating touchstones. If not honored, those items have the potential for becoming absolute "deal breakers." The other three items on the list become supporting

priorities. (You will keep all six items—honoring each of your needs—you're just prioritizing them by joint agreement.)

2. Together, describe in written detail what the three "biggies" you have jointly agreed upon mean to your partnership. Clearly outline the actions and activities pertinent to those items.

3. On a new sheet of paper, explain in outline form why each of your three top items is strategic to your united personal fulfillment and eternal happiness. The other three items will be treated as secondary but still important.

Talk—talk—talk. Unless each item is clearly defined, there is too much room for misunderstanding. Men are known for wanting to stop without this talking. Their take is often: "I don't need to be so clear; we understand what we mean by those words." That is a sure formula for misunderstandings—misunderstandings that can loom very large at some later time.

Step 3: Label Your Touchstones

When you have completed your statements, go outside and pick up three large stones and three smaller stones. Label the three bigger stones with words that identify each of the "unwilling to live withouts." Put them in a beautiful container. These are your Vision Stones. Now label and add the three secondary stones around the sides. We'll call these your Supporting Stones. If you've put the big ones in first, the smaller ones will easily fit.

For example, if you're not yet married, or are married but yours is not yet a temple marriage, and that is one of your "can't live without" priorities, label one of your Vision Stones as such and then gauge all your choices and actions accordingly. Perhaps another priority might be to have several children and raise them in the gospel. That certainly gives you a clear vision when looking for a mate, doesn't it?

Your Supporting Stones come next. They are really important—but not "deal breakers." A woman might say, "I have to marry a man who will travel and regularly take me to exotic places." A man might say, "I must marry a woman who will go out camping and to all the sports events with me and who is really, really trim." Would you *really* not marry unless you could find such a person? If that's the case, isn't it best to know that now?

If circumstances or health altered a spouse's ability to travel or to participate in active sports, or pregnancy caused her to gain and retain weight, would these be deal breakers? I would hope not. These are supporting priorities, and over the years, as circumstances dictate, they can be renegotiated.

As time goes on you can add even smaller stones, reflective of desired but smaller dreams, images, and plans. But remember, they're just "small stuff." If they go unrealized, don't let them become relationship disrupters. With this paring down and defining, each person in the relationship understands and accepts ownership of the vision.

It is helpful to keep a beautiful bowl with these rocks symbolizing your joint vision in a prominent place in your home. Pull them out and talk about them often. If there are children in the home, share your vision with them.

Does Your "Together Vision" Change?

It is intended that we grow in life and that we grow in marriage. As we grow, our vision emerges more clearly, reflecting where we are in our lives. Most growth comes in spurts, and both parties in a relationship will not grow in exactly the same way at the same time. Therefore, at every major phase of your life, it would be good to pull out your touchstones and see if it's time to replace them with new Vision or Supporting Stones that reflect the "biggies" of this next stage of your growth. What are the challenges you'll be facing in this segment of your life? What is your next mission, your next dream? It is time once again for each of you to prepare your own Vision Statements and then to combine them.

Perhaps you're feeling a need to give priority to your children's education or to furthering your own or your spouse's education. Is this the time to strike out on a new career, start your own business, or move to another locale? Is it time to look to fulfilling one of your big-ticket dream items, to find new ways to connect with children out of the home, to link your family forever through family history and temple work, or to work on your fitness and health? There are so many changes life will require of you, and so many new avenues for growing together.

It is important to remember that you can never have more than three big Vision Stones and three Supporting Stones in the bowl at any one time. That doesn't mean you won't have more dreams and plans or more things that you hope to do together. It does mean that you've agreed to be happy as those basic core needs are met, and that neither of you is dealing with unrealistic expectations.

The Three-Stone Principle in Action

I recently received a telephone call from a woman I knew only slightly. She and her husband had attended a sacrament meeting where I had been asked to speak on creating celestial partnerships. There she had heard me discuss the three-stone principle. She asked if she could tell me her story.

Her career was as a full-time mother and homemaker, but she also did mural painting and decorating to supplement their income. About two years prior to our conversation, her husband had begun traveling more in his job. They had found that this time apart had resulted in fewer and fewer shared interests and more and more separate activities. Their marriage was disintegrating. It seemed they were on two separate journeys, and the only times their paths crossed were when they had to discuss hot-button items such as bills, misbehaving children, and unmet needs.

They had drifted so far apart that they could find no avenue for discussion that didn't erupt into "I told you so" or "Why don't you ever . . ."? Before that Sunday they were discussing separation. After a long Saturday night of fighting and tears they decided to go to church together, something they seldom did anymore. They agreed to talk about how they felt afterwards.

They were amazed at the content of that sacrament meeting, which was directed entirely to making marriages whole and holy. They both felt the three-stone principle had been meant specifically for them. They stopped at an open area on the way home and picked up their three large and three smaller stones. They immediately began developing their own personal Vision Statements and then folded them into their joint Vision Statement.

She related that once this was completed they had new hope, a new plan, and a new way to join together with focus, purpose, and understanding. They had found common dialogue, common words, a common cause, a common dream, a common vision.

This dear woman was now very hopeful about the long-term potential for their marriage. They both recognized that they had a lot of work to do in fixing up and mending a relationship that had gone too long untended. But they now felt that they had been armed with a working formula.

Another woman, a young career woman of about twenty-six whom I'll call Cara, spoke with me of her frustration that she could find no man who measured up to her preset expectations. Yet she wanted to be married. Could I give her any advice? I shared this three-stone principle with her, suggesting that it would help her narrow down those things she absolutely could not live without in the man she married.

Cara called me not too long after that conversation and told me how she had changed her thought process based on her use of this tool. She had narrowed her list of some sixteen traits she wanted in the man she married to three "won't live withouts" and three secondary touchstone desires. With her new pared-down—but spiritually heightened—list, she was now dating two men whom she might have passed over previously. Cara said that she had found each to be delightful, fun, and having unplumbed depth. I received an e-mail some months later saying that she was now engaged to one of those men and ecstatically happy.

A divorced woman of thirty-three, after hearing me talk of this on a college campus, came up afterward and said, "If I'd understood this principle earlier I'd still be married rather than sitting in this class trying to figure out how to put my life back together."

My husband and I find there are major shifts in our lives about every five to seven years, and with the early Vision Stones securely in place, we can move on to others. We recently relabeled our stones. We find the "biggies" don't change much in principle, but they generally do shift in application. Our lives, like the lives of many Church members, center on three principal visions: family, partnership, and relationship with God and the covenants.

Pierce and I are probably at a very different place from where you are just now. Your lists may be more focused on children, careers, adventure, or exponential growth. We've already had the grand adventures; we've traveled the world; we've had challenging, trying, growing careers and ups and downs with finances and emotions. We now find ourselves at a lovely but unfamiliar new place.

We're semi-retired, so now we have more disposable time, less disposable income, a home in a new locale, and new health issues. All this can be an adventure—and challenging, too—and we have seen many of our friends struggling to get their footing in this climate of change. So we recognized that it was time to see what we each wanted to be in this next phase of our lives.

We made a date for our touchstone evening, starting with dinner at a favorite restaurant. After the main course, we each brought out our Vision Statements and began the process of discussing what we meant by what we had said. I had listed a desire to share more meaningful religious experiences. He had listed a desire to grow in the gospel. We combined these desires into one joint priority and labeled it Gospel Growth. Then, in our Defining Statement, we decided that this would include going to the temple more often, designing and following our own course of study for our family home evenings, and making a commitment to spend at least one long evening weekly really talking together about gospel concepts and principles. This was our contract *together.* Individually, he or I can take whatever classes we want on our own, participate in study groups, or design our own reading courses. We may even do some of those things together. But all that is a bonus.

As my second priority I listed, "Always have fresh experiences." His second desire was to spend more time at our Salt Lake City condo, and to have specific things planned to do while there. (Since we left the Washington, D. C., area, our main home has been in Arizona.) We condensed and combined these under the words "Keeping Diversity in Our Lives," and our Defining Statement indicated that this would include (as long as we're able) scheduling a major travel event each year, being at the condo for each change of season, and helping one another get our personal histories written while we were at the condo. Even if we're not able to do those specific things, it will not change our vision. We have both agreed that if that is the case, we will find other ways to honor this touchstone principle and keep freshness and diversity in our lives.

Finally, we had both listed elements of connectedness to family. We decided that our vision for this season of our lives was to be as accessible to our grandchildren as they wished, planning, sharing, visiting, and communicating regularly.

These are all such simple visions, but they reflect where we are in our lives and the desires of our hearts at this time. Had we not taken the time to carefully think through, articulate, and discuss our joint vision statement, I suspect we both would have been puzzled about what we could do for each other during this season of change, or even wondering why the other couldn't be more responsive and sensitive to our own needs and desires. But within our carefully articulated priorities, those matters worth "going to the mat for" become very clear.

Whether you are married or unmarried, the three-stone principle can work in your life. Do the work as outlined above and you will soon find yourself counting your blessings rather than recounting your disappointments.

CHAPTER 10

UNDERSTANDING
YOUR LOVE

~

Who's happiest in marriage? Is it the man or the woman? Most people would likely assume that it is the woman; however, polls show that men are often happier than women in marriage. One of the reasons for this, we are told, is that they are generally less driven by a quest for perfection in their homes and personal lives. Perhaps this is because they aren't as enmeshed in the details of the home and the lives of those around them. They are able to close their eyes to a large measure of personal and emotional chaos. They feel more in control of their lives and more accepting of the choices they have made than women do.

Ranking highest on most men's comfort scale are peace at home, time to pursue their own interests, and an acceptance of them as they are. This sounds like little to ask. However, if you are the woman, trying to keep everyone and everything functioning, meeting all emotional and physical needs, managing a myriad of details with no staff except a handful of reluctant and forgetful helpers, you may feel that your partner needs to move himself more into the "active participant" column.

A man who is focused on his own comfort scale—"I don't ask much; can't you just give me a little space and time to myself?"—will probably pay little attention to the pesky details of day-to-day home and family care, maintenance, and growth . . . details that a woman can rarely ignore. With such a focus he can walk past a full garbage pail for days. It might never occur to him to put a dish in the dishwasher. He cannot seem to understand why the floor is not a proper place for cast-off clothing.

Men often don't really see what's out of place, so they seldom feel much responsibility for straightening up, picking up, or restoring order, no matter how much their wives may need their help. When that is the case, peace at home is an elusive commodity.

Men work so hard outside the home that often they don't recognize the need to be more truly partners in the home. It would mean so much to their wives if they would assume complete—not reluctant—responsibility for certain tasks around the house. Speaking of hard work, a wife and mother's job has been measured as the equivalent of two full-time jobs. Add to this church responsibilities and the very real possibility of her holding a job outside the home—how can the math be made to work for any woman?

On the other hand, it is really wonderful that most men consider their wives their treasures and generally would change less about them than a woman would suspect. Recently I heard one of rock music's "bad boys" crediting his wife of two years for the dramatic turnabout that had taken place in his life. He used surprising and remarkable phrases. "Because of her, I have come closer to who I aspire to be," he said without guile. "I have changed because she makes it easier for me to talk to God." These are the traits most men are searching for in a love relationship. Isn't that the soul building we've been talking about? Aren't these the ennobling and life-altering gifts God intended us to give one to another?

When we were first married, Pierce would stop people on the street and say: "Look at this beautiful girl. Just look at her! Can you believe she married me?" I always blushed, felt totally uncomfortable, and tried to change the conversation as I sought to move quickly on. Now I recognize that gesture as the statement of delight in and affirmation of our relationship that it was. Let your husband find you wonderful. Don't insist that you aren't. In turn, find him wonderful. And then be wonderful together. Keep your ears and hearts open to the possibilities. Partnership is a forever commitment to holding each other precious and to keeping the flames of love bright. This will require active and loving thought by each of the signatories to the contract. Love, like fires, must always have new fodder.

The "Why I Married Him or Her" List

You are now ready to embark on another list of threes. Begin by calling to mind three wonderful things about your partner that enchanted and entranced you so totally that you believed he or she could make you happy here and in the eternities. Take time to record answers to the following questions.

The Beginning

1. What was it that made you laugh at and with one another?
2. Describe your happiest date—your happiest day.
3. Describe that one most incredible thing about your partner that caused you to see such wonderful potential for your union.

The Trust

1. What was it that you found in your partner to deem him or her worthy of entrusting yourself and your posterity to, through all eternity?
2. Describe an important deeply spiritual or personal moment between the two of you.
3. What is the most important spiritual thing you've learned from him or her?

The Here and Now

1. Name three important sights or sounds of your language together.
2. Given the gift of magic for one day, what would you do for your partner?
3. What is the greatest physical thing about your partner? The greatest spiritual thing?

Rehearse the positive answers in your mind. Believe in and place value on those qualities once again. Love that is believed in quickly becomes love that can be embraced. Virtues are like diamonds: You have to mine for them, but once found, they are forever valuable. Disappointment, on the other hand, has an even stronger corrosive power, and over time it will wear away the strongest of foundations.

Share your list with your companion. Then, after several months of reveling in those lists, select and record three more wonderful things about your partner. Every few months for the rest of your life, make these lists of "threes." Recycle ideas, if necessary, but keep them uppermost in your mind. Save them and reread them from time to time. Put your new list of threes in his briefcase, under her pillow, or as a bookmark in the book your partner is reading.

Relationships require time, attention, and nurturing. They can't be left to fend for themselves.

The Ebb and Flow of Love

Two people can get lazy in their relationship, especially if they have been married for a while. They can forget what it is to open their souls to each other. They can let inertia take away all that is beautiful in their marriage. It's important to remember that love is like a muscle in your body: You either use it or you lose it. And I'm not talking about the physical act of love—I'm talking about the mental aspects as well.

With trials, spurts of personal need, or searching for new direction, the emotions of married love ebb and flow like the ocean. People grow differently. There may even be periods in your marriage when you will feel like ships passing in the night, with one sinking and the other not hearing the S.O.S. At those times your joint vision, and your commitment to that vision, will become as a life raft. Hold on to it tightly, lest the waves and the buffeting toss one of you out into the raging sea.

Anton Chekhov said: "Any idiot can face a crisis. It's

day-to-day living that wears you out." That's the truth in marriage as well. Routine exposes the lows as well as the highs of
any relationship, the weaknesses as well as the strengths of any
individual. Conflicting desires, pressures of economics, disappointments in life and self, problems with children, career
demands, and a hundred other challenges will try the strongest
of bonds. At such times, the reasons for your love seem only
dimly visible—as if a line on a far horizon.

When this happens in your marriage, remind yourself that
you and your spouse are two different people and that each of
you is here to get a graduate degree in love and forgiveness in
order to become more like God. Here are some statements you
can focus on. Repeat them aloud to yourself, if that helps.

"We are both children of a loving God, created in His
image, and He loves us equally."

"He knew we would get through this."

"After the trial come the blessings."

"The Plan is perfect."

Then recount once again the reasons for your love and
commitment in the first place, and find new ways to share your
interests and your lives.

Allow yourself to be sensitive and to dream anew. Years of
hurt, both real and imagined, can build calluses on the heart. It
will take time for them to wear away, but remember that love
is the most powerful force in the universe, and love does beget
love. For each of us there is a time when there is more pain in
remaining "tight in a bud" than in opening our soul and allowing a new kind of love to blossom.

True oneness will not be found in a change of circumstances, only in a change of heart—yours. This ability to

change and grow in love and in the capacity to love is that very work for which partnerships were designed. As we come to know and place value on another's dignity, we embrace our own. As we learn what it means to put another first, as we learn about forgiveness and understanding, as we become helpers and saviors to each other in matters both physical and spiritual, we learn about extending lifelines, about selflessness, and about patience. As we strive to love with an infinite and perfect love, we come nearer to Godhood.

There are circumstances in which hearts have been broken, trust crushed, sensitivities trampled. When such has occurred, opening the heart and the soul becomes much more difficult. However, unless there are matters of concern for safety and self, I almost always advocate trying hard to put the marriage and the trust back together again. This will require courage, sacrifice of ego, and searching and commitment on the part of both participants. Spiritual and even professional counseling may be needed.

When vows have been broken, a long and very focused repentance process must be entered into, forgiveness must be genuine, and a new joint vision must be arrived at mutually.

Imprinted clearly on the sensory receptors of each partner in any marriage will need to be a vision of their marriage as a holy adventure that will return them, in oneness, to rule and reign in their Father's kingdom. The highest degree of glory can be accessed only with an eternal companion.

Without question, the richest love is that which surrenders itself to the judgment of time and all the eternities. We must never take our eyes off the prize. Do you think our pioneer forebears could ever have stood the trials of the trail if they had not steadfastly focused on the vision?

It is easy to fall in love. To stay in love, to grow in love, and to build on that love to create a family and home are some of mortality's greatest and most exhilarating challenges. And when those challenges are met, and we have lived our lives in honor of God's commands and covenants, we are promised kingdoms and principalities.

The secret of a "vision partnership" is to place value on your relationship and on each other. Praise wherever you can, love whenever you can, and counsel with one another always. Recognize your differences and factor them into the credit column and into your responses.

Have adequate job descriptions and do your own job with absolute goodwill and confidence. Pray together. Play together. Lighten up a bit; keep your sense of humor intact. Laugh together, and when the hard times come, as they surely will, cry together. Hold one another, your love, and your partnership as the most precious of God's gifts and keep your beloved always at the core of your relationship. Be ever aware that the purpose of this earthly life, with love and families and challenges, is to prepare us in wisdom and oneness, that we may press on in the next life to organize and manage worlds of our own.

Above all, learn to love one another in the present and allow that love to flow back to you—in the present, not at some faraway future time that may never come. Marriages die only when there are no dreams, when the pains outweigh the pleasure, when the work is too much and the wonder of each other is gone. The real challenge of marriage is to see that none of those things happen!

DISCUSSION BREAK

Here would be a good place to refer back to your list from the Introduction and seriously explore and commit to those three relationship issues you will address this coming year as individuals and as a partnership.

OF ROLES AND ONENESS

*So it is that the real but unheralded heroes
and heroines of our time are the men and women of the
earth who uncommonly resist the world's common
temptations, who surmount the common tribulations of the
world and continue to the very end in righteousness,
arriving home battered slightly, yet much bettered.*

—NEAL A. MAXWELL

CHAPTER 11

FATHERS: PURVEYING, PROVIDING, AND PROTECTING

It has been wisely said that *to become* a father is not difficult, but to *be* a father—ah—there's the challenge. With a culture reeling, with values shifting, with a society that often reduces the tasks of a father to providing financial support and showing up at a family event once in a while, some men are perplexed. They know in their hearts that there is much more to fatherhood than that. Many men are seeking a clearer perspective.

Based on the light found in the scriptures, the words of living prophets, and the examples of wise fathers I have known, I'd like to suggest three clear roles for all fathers to hold close.

Role Number 1: Purveyor of Knowing and Being

Nephi begins the record of his people with these words: "I, Nephi, having been born of goodly parents, therefore I was taught somewhat in all the learning of my father" (1 Nephi 1:1). Enos credited his father for his teachings, "knowing my father that he was a just man—for he taught me in his language, and also in the nurture and admonition of the Lord—and blessed be the name of my God for it" (Enos 1:1).

Fatherhood is about passing on knowledge, but, most important, it's about passing on wisdom and life lessons. In his early years, a son's sense of self depends on his father's demonstrating to him that he sees him as a "beloved son, in whom he is well pleased."

Fathers know what the layers of the earth are called, what the ages of man are, how to chart the stars in the heavens. And, to the delight of children and particularly of preteen sons, they seem to know the names of—and all else about—anything that has wheels, that involves a ball of some sort, that crawls, swims, climbs, or flies, or to which the "stats" apply.

Fatherhood is about passing on that knowledge, but, most important, it's about passing on wisdom and life lessons. We learn from studies that in his early years, a son's sense of self depends on his father's demonstrating to him that he sees him as a "beloved son, in whom he is well pleased" (see Matthew 3:17). The need for that kind of affirmation from his earthly father is as important to a son as is our need for that selfsame affirmation from our Heavenly Father.

We also learn that in the teen years this son needs to know that his father trusts him enough to allow him to try on his "intrepid adventurer" role—while at the same time feeling secure that his father will reel him back if he gets too far out. And finally, we learn that in his young adult years a son will find it difficult to become sensitively attuned to the nuances of relationships and to trust himself to a deep and committed love if he has never seen this in his father.

We speak often of the importance of fathers to sons—and it is not just significant but critical. However, a father's importance to daughters is equally crucial. One father I spoke with made the following observation: "We sell our daughters and ourselves short when we reduce our definition of provider to a paycheck. Our daughters need our presence, experience, masculinity, nurturing, challenge, affection, and support—things paychecks can't buy."

Generally a father is his daughter's first real love, the model by which she will measure all other men who enter her life—for good or for ill. Through watching their fathers, daughters learn how to judge most relationships and how to respond in them. So a father needs to be very aware of the example he sets.

My father was particularly good at being a father. I remember when I was a little girl my father would invite me into the fruit orchards as the apple trees were coming into full blossom, and there we would revel in the sweet, pungent smell. From his prunings he would fashion a corsage for me, hum a waltz, and encourage me to feel beautiful and to dance with grace and elegance. I saw later that he was teaching me the way I should feel about myself and the way I should expect boys to treat me.

It was my father who bought me the red velvet dress at Christmastime, so impractical and expensive—but so desired—and by that act I internalized the message that I was deserving of occasional treats of beauty.

In our rides to and fro he taught me to play a game he called "When Our Ship Comes In." In this game, if we could dream a thing—and if we could explain what that dream would entail—we were entitled to believe that it would be ours someday. And he didn't just have me articulate my dreams, he shared his with me. I learned it was all right to keep striving and growing and believing because here was this man, successful in the ways of man and God—a man who everyone I knew seemed to think was wonderful—and he still had unfulfilled dreams.

Generally a father is his daughter's first real love, the model by which she will measure all other men who enter her life— for good or for ill.

Because of this, I have seldom been afraid to dream or to try on any of life's larger scenarios. A father's very presence allows a daughter to think: "The boundaries of my world are secure. I can now trust and love and grow."

The story is told of an elementary school teacher who had students write essays in hopes that it would motivate the fathers to attend a PTA meeting. The fathers came in their BMWs, their SUVs, their minivans, and their pickup trucks. Their occupations were varied: CEOs, lawyers, construction supervisors, laborers, teachers. Each father identified himself somewhat in terms of occupation, financial worth, charm, looks, and personal worthiness.

The teacher greeted these fathers and then randomly selected the essays to be read: "I like my daddy," read one. "He put my bike together and ran behind me while I learned to ride." The others were similar. "I like my daddy . . . he shoots hoops with me all the time . . . he thinks I can make beautiful things . . . he watches me dance . . . he helps me learn to read . . . he holds me high up so I can see things . . . he sings in the car when we go on trips . . . he laughs so loud that it makes me feel happy inside." Not one child mentioned the father's occupation, the family house, car, neighborhood, food, or clothing.

Another key sort of "knowing" that fathers convey to their children is the knowledge of how to sacrifice in God's name, how to look to a higher standard to live by. Generations in my own family line have been influenced by pages from the journal of my Grandfather Samuel Richard Brough, and other journals and histories that recount some of his activities. In them we have learned of the reality and the reach of such sacrifice. Let me relate just a few events.

After four years as a missionary in England, where he presided over the Welsh, Irish, and Scottish Mission, Samuel was at last able to return to his wife and family. He records: "Before I arrived home from the mission field, I sold my last horse, also my stock (except for a few cows for the family's use) and used every dollar in my mission account." There was nothing left of what had been considerable holdings.

Needing to start anew, he traveled to the Bridger Valley of Wyoming and after a four-day search located the land he thought would serve him well for the remainder of his years. He immediately filed a homestead on 160 acres and moved his family to that barren area. He began life there by going to the mountains, hewing down enormous trees, loading them on a wagon pulled by only two horses, and hauling those trees to a spot where he could trim and split them into lumber for the construction of a home.

Over a period of time his fields flourished and he built two beautiful homes for himself and many others for the "settlers." A newspaper of the period reports that "the first crop of oats shipped out of Bridger Valley was raised by Mr. S. R. Brough. They are the best we've ever received." The valley continued to grow and prosper in its own modest way, as did Samuel.

With growth came a need to organize an official town and ward, and to create the office of bishop. Samuel, who had been the presiding elder, was called to that position. On May 9, 1899, Elders Francis M. Lyman and Abraham Woodruff traveled to this valley to determine where the town site would be. After traveling throughout the area and listening to the many groups of affected citizens, it was left for the Apostles to decide on the town site. It is recorded: "Elder Lyman announced that his choice fell upon Bishop Samuel Richard Brough's homestead, which was beautifully situated on high ground overlooking nearly the entire country. Bishop Brough, to whom the choice was a surprise, explained, with tears in his eyes, that he had become very much attached to his homestead, and he explained that nothing but the advice and desire of the Apostles could induce him to part with it. For the benefit of the people, however, he would let it go freely." His personal journal entry of May 9, 1899, reads: "I have never wept before when the Lord has asked me to give up anything—but tonight I did. I poured my heart out to the Lord and by morning my soul was at peace."

He did not let this claiming of his land interrupt his service or his testimony in any way. He continued as bishop, serving a total of twenty years. He was a leader in all the public enterprises, and through his advice—and often with his means—assisted many in getting homes and was principal in building most of the businesses that make a town work. At one time he had lumber and other materials on the ground to build himself a home, but let it all go to the building of a meetinghouse.

President Baxter, a member of his stake presidency, records of another time: "In company with President Tingey I was on my way to Manila, when we called at Lyman and found Bishop Brough in the midst of his harvest. He was standing on a wheat stack, stacking grain from four or five wagons, with the perspiration streaming down his face. I looked up to him and said, 'Bishop, we are going to Manila and would like you to accompany us.' He said: 'Well, you see how I am situated, but if you say "go" I will go.' When I said 'go,' he climbed down off the stack, put another man in his place and accompanied us to Manila, which trip took us three days."

This father in Zion will ever stand to his posterity as the standard by which we must conduct our lives.

Role Number 2: Provider of Bread and Dreams

Husbands and fathers are multifaceted, deeply caring partners. Their finer instincts and generous souls bring depth and breadth to a relationship. They generally come bearing deep love coupled with pragmatism and practicality. Their eyes often see beyond that which is obvious, to the possibilities and potential.

Our leaders have taught us that the most important thing a father can do for his children is to love their mother. They have also taught that it is primarily the father's role to provide for his family. It is because of the first, the love for his wife, that a husband finds the heavy load of providing to be more joy than burden.

A man is not a failure if he cannot provide all the commodities his family might desire. It isn't easy to fully supply a home or to give everyone in the family what they want in the way of clothes, trips, and "things."

Most men perceive themselves as the primary breadwinner and in fact should be so. It's important in this equation, though, for all to understand that a man is not a failure if he cannot provide all the commodities his family might desire. It isn't easy to fully supply a home or to give everyone in the family what they want in the way of clothes, trips, and "things." The wife and children, recognizing this load, should do their best to live within the scope of the resources brought into the home.

Remember, unrealistic expectations are a major cause of unhappiness in marriages and families. Families should avoid such unhappiness at every turn. Each partner, along with the children, will likely end up—at least in the early years—having to creatively make do. Sometimes even simple wishes will have to make way for basic necessities. This may well mean that all in the family will have to rein in their desires.

You may not have sufficient resources to have a home that feels large enough or decorated enough. You may not have all the toys or sports or adventures you would like. Your children may not have all the electronics and designer clothes their friends have. Families need to carefully and cooperatively consider what kinds of activities and possessions will be economically feasible for them. All, including children, should respect and express appreciation for that which each partner contributes to the creating of their home.

This division of labor, the role of outside provider being equal with the responsibilities of a full-time mother in the home, is in the interests of the integrity of the family. Often the reason for the woman working outside of the home, however, is that such a provider is not available, is not able, or is not willing to carry the basic load.

A sobering statistic with which women are faced—and with which all of society's organizations must deal—is that 90 percent of women will work outside the home for some portion of their lives, and more than half of those will be the primary breadwinners at some time. This is a stark reminder that a woman should place significant priority on getting her education in a field that will allow her to enter the marketplace as necessary, and at a level that will allow her to live and work with dignity and pride. It would seem wise for most women to keep skills polished and updated throughout their lives. Husbands and children should give full support to such an undertaking.

Whatever the reason for a woman's working outside the home, full recognition should be given for her contributions. Such a woman should feel pride in her work, and no one should judge or attempt to assign any feelings of guilt because she cannot be at home full time.

Role Number 3: Protector of Body and Soul

Barbara Walters of television's *20/20* did a story on gender roles in Kabul, Afghanistan, several years before the Afghan conflict. She noted that women customarily walked five paces behind their husbands. She recently returned to Kabul and observed that women, despite the overthrow of the oppressive Taliban regime, seem to walk even farther behind their husbands—and seemed happy about it.

Ms. Walters approached one of the Afghan women and asked, "Why do you now seem happy with the old custom that you once tried so desperately to change?" The woman looked Ms. Walters straight in the eyes and, without hesitation, said, "Land mines." The moral of the story, according to Ms. Walters, was, "Behind every man is a very smart woman." But I think it's much more than that—in front of that very smart women is a hero/protector.

An American girl who had never known her father asked her mother what he was like. The mother responded: "I once took a car trip with your father. Back roads all the way from Chicago to Detroit. It was a blizzard. The snow was coming down like chicken feathers and we got stuck. It was in the middle of nowhere. I thought we would freeze to death that night. But you know what he did? He unbuttoned his coat and I got inside with him. We were together in one coat. They said if we hadn't worn the one coat, we might have died. That's what I always think of when I think of your father" (Flook, *More*, 127–28).

We've talked earlier about man's desire to be a "hero," particularly to those he loves. We also explored his interest in adventure and danger, and recognized that much of this interest stems from a deep-rooted and strongly felt knowing that he would be "put to the test." Most men do not remember why this would be so, nor do they recognize that they came to earth knowing full well that the grandest test, the most heroic adventure, and the most dangerous challenge they would take on would be their fight for love, for family, and for God.

Yes, the father is intended to be the protector of the home in every way. He guards it against the intrusion of evil from without. Formerly he protected his home with a variety of locks and barred windows. Today the task is more complex. Although locked doors and secured windows may protect against physical invasion, protecting the family against the invasion of evil is not so easy. Turn on a computer, and evil can creep through even the most innocuous web sites. A television, unless carefully monitored, allows mind-warping stimuli, difficult to anticipate, to permeate the space before you can even change the channel.

Satan does desire to usurp your children's minds and bodies, perhaps even more than he desires yours—and he will use every advancement of modern technology to do so. In our day, there is no more need for him to knock down the door.

Satan does desire to usurp your children's minds and bodies, perhaps even more than he desires yours—and he will use every advancement of modern technology to do so. In our day, there is no more need for him to knock down the door.

And that bring us to that most important role of a father, as protector of the soul. Fathers in Zion are sensitive to the gospel and take their duties very seriously. They understand that they are to teach the gospel to their families, that they are to hold regular family home evenings. They get up early to drive the children to seminary and often lead out in family prayer. They know they are to help prepare their children for missions and temple marriages. As patriarchs in their homes, they exercise their priesthood by performing the appropriate ordinances for their families and by giving blessings to their wives and children—and what a blessing that is!

Further understanding of the importance of a father in the home is brought into focus by the following statistics as reported by Harbinger Press:

90% of homeless and runaway children are from fatherless homes.

71% of pregnant teenagers lack a father.

63% of youth suicides are from fatherless homes.

85% of children who exhibit behavioral disorders come from fatherless homes.

We are in a national crisis relating to fathers. One estimate from the National Fatherhood Initiative claims that "25 million children live absent their biological father." And, after divorce, nearly 50 percent of children never see their fathers again.

Seeing what the absence of a father in the home does to the hearts, minds, souls, and lives of precious children, we will all perhaps place greater value on the father's role. Whoever you are—give your most heartfelt thanks to that father who is being a father.

CHAPTER 12

UNITY IN THE
WORK

~~~

Marriage relationships are not the only partnerships for which we are designed. Apart from marriage, there are deep friendships, there are families and extended families, there are Church relationships and responsibilities, coalitions, community organizations . . . oh so many ways of forming "partnerships"—of interacting with and valuing one another.

No discussion of men and women and partnerships would be complete without some dialogue regarding our oneness as we come together as a Zion people. Indeed, outside the family, there is no greater school for unity than our participation in our Church activities and our work in our Church callings.

We know that the Church, its offices, and its programs were established by a loving God that there might be a place where we could come together, male and female, as a community of believers to support, sustain, teach, lead, sacrifice for, and find joy in one another. Here we find common cause and sanctuary as we learn the principles, doctrines, and ordinances of His kingdom. It is as we participate in these activities and as we magnify our callings that we move onto that advanced training ground God has designed where His imperfect daughters and sons can begin working toward perfection.

Let me assure you that there is no difference in the importance to the Church of men compared with women, although their roles and assignments do differ, and this difference is part of "divine design."

Of Equal Import

From the outside looking in, there are some who suggest that men's importance to the Church goes unquestioned, whereas the import of women to the work is not clear. President Gordon B. Hinckley has related that as he goes about the country, media representatives ask often in accusatory tones about this. He responds: "I know of no other organization in all the world which affords women so many opportunities for development, for sociality, for the accomplishment of great good, for holding positions of leadership and responsibility" ("Women of the Church," 67).

Let me assure you that there is no difference in the importance to the Church of men compared with women, although their roles and assignments do differ, and this difference is part of "divine design." Speaking to the women of the Church, President J. Reuben Clark Jr. said that from the time Christianity was established until the present, "woman has comforted and nursed the Church. She has borne more than half the burdens, she has made more than half the sacrifices, she has suffered the most of the heartaches and sorrows.

"In the modern Church hers has been the abiding, unquestioning faith, the pure knowledge, that has enheartened the Priesthood and kept it going forward against all odds. Her loving trust, her loyal devotion were the faithful anchor that held when storms were fiercest" (in Conference Report, April 1940, 21). As President Heber J. Grant stated: "Without the wonderful work of the women I realize that the Church would have been a failure" (*Gospel Standards,* 150).

Our women's church work has not just been in the traditionally feminine fields of teaching Sunday School and relieving the poor. From the beginning, Mormon women have regularly preached and prayed from the pulpit, served as missionaries, and filled leadership positions. It thus becomes apparent that God wishes the women, as well as the men, to focus on a full and positive role, with attendant responsibility, in the Church. It would appear that he would like both men and women to fully understand the equality of their service in his eyes, though that service may go by different names. He would like us to be aware of and take pride in the unique and individual nature of our assignments. He would like us ultimately to recognize the immense responsibility we have for the growth of our own souls.

"This makes individuals of men and women—individuals with the right of free agency, with the power of individual decision, with individual opportunity for everlasting joy, whose own actions throughout the eternities, with the loving aid of the Father, will determine individual achievement. There can be no question in the Church of man's rights versus woman's rights. They have the same and equal rights" (Widtsoe, *Evidences and Reconciliations*, 305).

Men and women of every age should feel joyful and active responsibility for the substantive functioning of the Church's programs and for the upholding and expounding of its principles.

But What If You Really Are Feeling Undervalued?

At times, however, some women have expressed to me that they really do feel marginalized and dismissed, with their work in the Church being absorbed or usurped by others who make no attempt to be inclusive or unified. At the same time, there are some men who feel that they are overworked and that their enormous contributions of time and talent are undervalued. Although such feelings may at times be valid, the hurt that causes them is generally not intended. It's just that the work of the Church is being carried out by mere mortals. None of us come to the body of Christ without imperfections and blind spots; yet an ever generous Lord will use us regardless of our imperfections, as long as we are willing to be used.

None of us come to the body of Christ without imperfections and blind spots; yet an ever generous Lord will use us regardless of our imperfections, as long as we are willing to be used.

Elder Joseph B. Wirthlin has taught us: "The Church is not a place where perfect people gather to say perfect things, or have perfect thoughts, or have perfect feelings. The Church is a place where imperfect people gather to provide encouragement, support, and service to each other. . . . We are here with the same purpose: to learn to love Him with all our heart, soul, mind and strength, and to love our neighbor as ourselves" ("The Virtue of Kindness," 28).

We are called to magnify our callings without magnifying ourselves. All of us spend a lifetime learning one lesson at a time, some from a primer, and some from the graduate syllabus. Most everyone is just doing the best he or she can.

I recall a particularly challenging, and in many ways defining, moment in my Church life. Married, with children in assorted grades of junior high and high school, we were finishing a new home. My husband was enmeshed in his career, and my own work was unusually demanding. I was also stake Young Women president. Happy? Amidst the juggling, all my dreams were being realized. Time, as ever, was the challenge. I could keep all current balls in the air, but the balance was precarious. One misstep and they would all crash about me in chaos. I'm sure every woman and most men can understand that feeling.

As a Young Women board we had decided that the girls of our stake needed and would benefit significantly from a particular series of events. This program had been designed, presented, and properly cleared. There were several physical and logistical problems, which required someone outside of our regular contact line to interact with us. This brother was not interested in the program, and when we needed to arrange for details he was unavailable, uncooperative, and unsupportive. When you are going the extra mile, so to speak, someone else's lack of cooperation or negativity seems to be even more emotionally and spiritually exhausting to you.

After trying all that I knew, I requested an appointment

with my stake president. I had carefully condensed the information I would present, so that I might not use too much of his time. I explained once again why the programs were important, what we would accomplish, and the mechanics involved, and then explained the problem.

My method of handling problems had always been direct. I had expected his action to be equally quick and decisive. Just one phone call from him could fix the whole problem, I thought. Instead he said, "My dear, you go back and love him through this."

I left his office feeling exhausted, discouraged, and a bit put upon. I certainly did not have time for such sensitive steering through the shoals. There were too many others in my circle of life who needed my considered and thoughtful attention.

In my home that night, after all my charges were secure and my duties completed, I fell to my knees and poured out my frustrations to the Lord, explaining what needed to be done. Surely our priesthood leaders felt the same concern for their daughters as they did for their sons, I remember thinking. As the night wore on I weighed all the options and decided that, as important as this seemed, perhaps the only sensible answer was to cancel the entire set of programs. My mind churned on, and before I realized it I was reviewing other hurts and slights, real and imagined, that I had suffered in my Church callings.

Awakening from a restless half-sleep, I became aware of a darkness descending in the room. I knew what it was. It was the presence of the adversary. Through my dejection and frustration, righteous though I felt it was, I had opened the door just a crack. He, seizing every opportunity available to him, had flung it wide open and had entered, planning to use this moment to his advantage. My beloved husband, whose priesthood powers I relied on so totally, was traveling. He was not there to hold me in his arms, pray with me, and dispel this evil influence.

Knowing God's personal promises of power over the adversary, I used the power of prayer and invoked the promised protection through the name of the Savior, commanding that the adversary leave. The blackness in the room gradually dissipated; however, the blackness that permeated my mind stayed.

The following day was Saturday. I could barely function, so completely had my senses been overwhelmed with this darkness. Prayer helped, but not enough. My children and the day's home activities helped, but not enough. It wasn't until I got out into the sunlight, away from all darkness, that I could once again begin to see clearly. I returned home and again knelt in prayer. However, this time I was not telling the Lord what He had to do. I was asking Him to forgive me for my wavering spirit. I then asked Him what I needed to do.

By Sunday I was on an even spiritual and emotional keel, much humbled, and seeking to be part of a Christlike solution. I felt impressed that it would be wise to approach this dear brother, who was probably as overwhelmed with the demands of his life as I was with mine, and ask him, "How can I help you? How can I make it easier to accomplish what we need?"

Those were the right questions. Out of his mouth poured his own frustrations. He spoke of the demands on his time and his feeling that this was just another unnecessary "add-on." We were able to talk it through and work matters out. The programs were a success, and he became one of our greatest allies.

There are few men I've talked with who have not felt similarly overburdened by the tasks of life, home, fatherhood, and their priesthood callings. I'm so grateful the Lord led this good brother and me to a solution of the problem. Man or woman, we can accomplish so much more if we will just try to be more sensitive to one another.

I am firmly convinced that our participation in the Church, in our individual wards and stakes, just as in our homes, is designed to help us grow in all ways important to our lives and to our exaltation.

Emerging Wiser and More in Touch with the Spirit

Why did that experience happen to me at that particular time in my life? I'm not sure. But I do know that every lesson I learned was one I would call upon later as a touchstone for spiritual direction. I emerged wiser, more in tune with the Lord, more aware of my absolute reliance on Him. I also recognized the reality and power of Satan as never before, and the need to be ever cautious of criticisms and judgments.

Seldom a week goes by that the words of that wise and gentle stake president do not ring in my ears: "Just love him into it." I confess, I have to keep relearning that same lesson, but when all else has failed, that is the tape that plays over and over in my head. That is the answer that comes after my prayers.

My husband and I were touring Nauvoo and Carthage, Illinois, with our grandchildren. As we visited Carthage Jail, our hearts were torn by the recounting of that infamous day of carnage. We came out into the sunlight of the plaza to find our eyes immediately drawn to D. J. Bawden's sculpture of Joseph and Hyrum, entitled *The Martyrs.* In silent reflection we contemplated their unwavering loyalty, one to the other, as they were mercilessly killed at the hands of a raging mob with blackened faces.

In this remarkable statue, Hyrum, the older brother, stands a bit to the back and yet beside Joseph. His right hand is on Joseph's shoulder and his left hand is on his arm, supporting and sustaining and bearing him up, looking with him steadfastly into the future. He is strong, unwavering, loving, and loyal. "In life they were not divided, and in death they were not separated" (D&C 135:3). This statue will ever stand in my mind as the picture of how we support one another in the Church.

I am firmly convinced that our participation in the Church, in our individual wards and stakes, just as in our homes, is designed to help us grow in all ways important to our lives and to our exaltation. I learned in my years of working with the Brethren that there was no place for contention, only positive solution. They have been thus schooled by the Lord, and know that His Spirit will not abide where there is disharmony, ill will, fault finding, or criticism, even though seemingly deserved. I have learned that one of the greatest lessons God is trying to teach us is oneness: to learn to move in perfect harmony, goodwill, and trust.

CHAPTER 13

SHARING THE LOAD, OR, WHO'S SCHEDULING FAMILY HOME EVENING?

~

I am often asked: "How do we, as a partnership, translate Church programs, roles, and responsibilities into an active working model in the home?" One young wife told me, only half-jokingly, that if family home evenings were to be held in their home, she had to do all the planning, call the children together, pull her husband away from his computer, and then tell him that everything was ready so he could preside.

Amidst the laughter I sensed her underlying feeling of frustration and even guilt. Was something wrong with her that the "ideal pattern" was not being played out in her home? Was it right for her to carry so much of the load to make these programs a part of their ongoing family life? And if all this was expected of her, why wasn't she being given a little more control and credit?

Yes, in the ideal situation the priesthood holder will lead out in implementing all of the wonderful safeguard programs that are so much a part of our religion: the family home evenings, family prayer, temple attendance, and so on. But in reality, all of the above becomes work of the partnership.

Elder Neal A. Maxwell recognized that "ideal" is a bit like "fair"; it doesn't always happen. He advised: "Malfunctioning fathers are a much more common phenomenon in the Church than are malfunctioning mothers. Often the success-oriented male leaves untended some of his responsibilities to his wife and family. . . . Having one 'sentry' who has gone AWOL joined by another 'sentry,' the wife and mother, is no help" (*Deposition of a Disciple*, 84).

And therein lies the answer. As a mother in Zion, would you deny yourself, your home, or your family any of the needed and available blessings? You are a full and equal partner. If a child needs a father's blessing, suggest it. If family prayer is being sidetracked, reinstitute it. If family home evenings are going to be fun, you know you can make it happen. Involve your husband as much as you can. Kidnap him if need be—but turn it into a positive rather than a negative experience. Pencil a temple date into his calendar and make it just that—a date. Soon he'll get the spirit of it.

As a mother in Zion, would you deny yourself, your home, or your family any of the needed and available blessings? You are a full and equal partner.

Opt for the greater good regardless of who gets the credit. The happiest relationships are those in which each partner is motivated by and acts with a mind-set that assures that both will emerge victorious. The operative principle should be, "If you don't win, I don't win." In marriage, more than in any other relationship, it gains you nothing if you win the battle and lose the war.

The bottom line, as you know, is that the real work for a woman is to get all those in her caring network back home safely. Woman acted as a savior by giving life to waiting spirits. Now she "saves" by seeing that all the saving programs of the gospel are resident in her home and are as fully implemented as possible.

"Accommodating" in a Priesthood Partnership

Presiding, providing, and protecting in a Latter-day Saint home are inseparably tied to priesthood gifts, shared responsibilities, and equitable partnership. Properly understood, exercised, and honored, these concepts create a truly Christlike environment in which all can grow and flourish.

The First Presidency advised the world of our beliefs and intentions, attributes and responsibilities in this regard: "By divine design, fathers are to preside over their families in love and righteousness and are responsible to provide the necessities of life and protection for their families. Mothers are primarily responsible for the nurture of the children. In these sacred responsibilities, fathers and mothers are obligated to help one another as equal partners" ("The Family: A Proclamation").

Marriage should and must be a full partnership, with the husband presiding, not ruling, in the home. How else could the principle of agency and freedom of choice operate for women? How could the principles of happiness be applied?

To hold and exercise the priesthood carries with it awesome responsibilities, for it is to be exercised only by righteous men who follow after the order of Adam, restored through Joseph Smith, under the direction of the Savior, who received the keys from God the Father. We will wish to pay heed to those ringing cautions set forth in the Doctrine and Covenants: "No power or influence can or ought to be maintained by virtue of the priesthood" (D&C 121:41).

Marriage should and must be a full partnership, with the husband presiding, not ruling, in the home. How else could the principle of agency and freedom of choice operate for women?

Although some men remain uninformed or misdirected in this regard, I believe the majority of men who hold the priesthood are more inclined, rather than less, to develop a wholly supportive and accommodating relationship of equality within their marriages. The word *accommodating* is best defined as being obliging, supportive, willing to adapt oneself to the other person's convenience. President Boyd K. Packer, speaking at a priesthood commemoration fireside, addressed this issue as relates to the partnership between husband and wife:

"It was not meant that the woman alone accommodate herself to the priesthood duties of her husband or her sons. She is of course to sustain and support and encourage them.

"Holders of the priesthood, in turn, must accommodate themselves to the needs and responsibilities of the wife and mother. Her physical and emotional and intellectual and cultural well-being and her spiritual development must stand first among his priesthood duties.

"There is no task, however menial, connected with the care of babies, the nurturing of children, or with the maintenance of the home that is not his equal obligation" ("Tribute to Women," 75).

Men who hold the priesthood are admonished to be persuasive, long-suffering, gentle, and meek, to be kind, and to show love unfeigned (see D&C 121). It seems almost superfluous to point out that a wife should exhibit those same traits in the partnership.

Individual Responsibility for Spiritual Light

While oneness in a marriage is essential, there are times when individuals must assume full responsibility for their own growth in a variety of ways. One of these is our own spiritual relationship with God the Father, with his Son, Jesus Christ, and with the Holy Ghost.

The Prophet Joseph Smith, upon turning the key in behalf of women to organize the Relief Society officially, proclaimed, "The Church was never perfectly organized until the women were thus organized" (Dahl and Cannon, *Encyclopedia of Joseph Smith's Teachings*, 537). At that time he told the women gathered that knowledge, intelligence, and the gifts of the Spirit would flow down to them.

Think of the last time you were on an airplane. As it began to taxi out onto the runway, you were instructed by the flight attendant that in the event of an emergency you were to put on your own oxygen mask first. Why are we to direct attention to ourselves first when there are others for whom we have responsibility? The answer is obvious: If we are to be able to help others survive, we must first assure our own survival. This principle carries itself out in nature as well: Were you aware that when the body is attacked, the heart pumps blood to itself first?

Without careful attention to our own spiritual, emotional, and physical health, we will be of little use in a situation that requires interdependence. The paradox is that, although unity is the higher law, it is predicated on confidence in our own individuality and independence, on our own loving, trusting, caring, believing relationship with the Father and the Son. Individually, we are responsible for asking the Holy Ghost to walk our daily walk with us and to be ever present in our lives. We are frequently reminded that the time is soon coming when no man or woman can rely on another's light.

Individually, we are responsible for asking the Holy Ghost to walk our daily walk with us and to be ever present in our lives.

This does not mean we will not reach out for insight and guidance and the shared learning and priesthood blessings of a supportive partnership. But, in the end, the vision, the plan, and the details of each person's own spiritual growth rests on his or her own shoulders, separate and distinct from the partnership.

So, to return to our original question: "How do we, as a partnership, translate Church programs, roles, and responsibilities into an active working model in the home?" The answer is that we must work together, accommodating each other's needs and gifts, and we must also work individually to fulfill our destiny as our Heavenly Father's covenant children.

CHAPTER 14

TWO BEINGS—
ONE PLAN

In the Prologue we discussed the Creation and learned that the entire reason the earth was created and the assignment given to tame and subdue, to civilize and contain was that there might be a place and a space of time where those who wished the privilege of claiming mortal bodies could come. Here they would be tested and tried, feel love and pain, know joy and sorrow, learn right and wrong, learn of the covenants, claim the promises for themselves, their marriages, and their families, and through the saving power and grace of Jesus Christ return glorified to their heavenly home.

Adam and Eve and all men and women to follow after them were given astounding and heroic assignments in this regard. Woman was given the sacred and miraculous responsibility of bringing life into the world—with the prospect that she may lose her life in that process. Man was given the holy and awesome responsibility of protecting life—and in that act may be required to give his life as well.

This concept of risking one's life to save another was key to the Garden experience. Eating of the fruit of the tree of knowledge of good and evil, forbidden to Adam and Eve only if they wished to stay in the Garden, entailed a sure physical death and the possibility of a spiritual death as well. It seems heaven's choices are often about life and death, all directed toward one final promise: eternal life.

Singly Important—Together Indomitable

In the Garden, God walked and talked with both Adam and Eve, passing on knowledge and wisdom necessary to bring the purposes of heaven to an earthly sphere. We understand this more clearly as we learn that the name *Adam* when used scripturally means the two of them, Adam and Eve—or Mr. and Mrs. Adam. It is only when the scriptures say specifically "the man Adam" that God is being exclusive—not inclusive. This lesson is important, as it relates to all messages coming from God, from the scriptures, and from our leaders: They're for both men and women. Though men and women may have individual assignments, they have a joint mission.

God allowed Satan into the Garden in order that there might be a choice to make, for, as we learn in 2 Nephi 2:16, "man could not act for himself save it should be that he was enticed by the one or the other." Once the need for a choice became apparent, God left Adam and Eve on their own with the hope that they would choose the greater law over the lesser law. That is God's hope for us. God trusts us to choose the greater law and to use the knowledge we gain from the tree of knowledge of good and evil to enlighten and benefit our lives.

Adam's response, when asked by God what he has done, gives us our first real look at the difference in the way men and women think. Adam says, in essence, "I did what I was supposed to do." Adam (man) was evidently hardwired from the beginning to reflect the black and white of a matter as he saw and understood it.

Woman was given the sacred and miraculous responsibility of bringing life into the world—with the prospect that she may lose her life in that process. Man was given the holy and awesome responsibility of protecting life—and in that act may be required to give his life as well.

Eve's thought process reflected an entire set of networking responsibilities: "If there is no other way that humankind can claim mortal bodies, then I will partake." We see care and concern (mercy), as expressed by Eve's thoughts and actions, moving in parallel with a story of right and wrong (justice) essential to Adam's mission. It becomes clear that both traits are essential and complementary, to be used together in wisdom, for the greatest good of all humankind.

As discussed in earlier sections, this dialogue not only gives us important information about how each of our brains and emotions are designed to work but makes it clear that we are expected to recognize and embrace the difference.

Without question, there are many tasks, activities, and careers in which both men and women can, and should, follow similar paths. Traits of strength, faith, and love are much alike. Yet, as it was with Eve, women have been sent to bring our uniquely created minds and mercy to the table, whether in the home or in the workplace. We do so without apology.

It is not women's mission to think, act, or prioritize as do men. Women's assignments are uniquely powerful and have awesome consequence. An oft-quoted truth is that there is but a twenty-year span between barbarism and civilization for any society. Why? Because that is all the time we have to teach our children our language, our values, our culture, and the importance of meaningful relationships. That is all the time we have to teach these precious builders of tomorrow's society our religion, our rites, and our concepts of agency and freedom; to see that education is advanced, that homes are havens, careers accommodating, and the national discourse focused and purposeful.

President Spencer W. Kimball spoke to this concept as he reminded men and women that, along with great assurances of equality, our roles and assignments do differ, and that such differences are eternal differences, "with women being given many tremendous responsibilities of motherhood and sisterhood and the men the tremendous responsibilities of fatherhood and the priesthood" (*My Beloved Sisters*, 37). We are told that in the world before we came here faithful women were given certain

An oft-quoted truth is that there is but a twenty-year span between barbarism and civilization for any society. Why? Because that is all the time we have to teach our children our language, our values, our culture, and the importance of meaningful relationships.

assignments while faithful men were foreordained to certain priesthood tasks.

President Kimball cautions that "while we do not now remember the particulars, this does not alter the glorious reality of what we once agreed to. We are accountable for those things which long ago were expected of us just as are those whom we sustain as prophets and apostles" (ibid.).

As to women's place in marriage, President Kimball said: "When we speak of marriage as a partnership, let us speak of marriage as a *full* partnership. We do not want our LDS women to be *silent* partners or *limited* partners in that eternal assignment! Please be a *contributing* and *full* partner" (ibid., 31; emphasis in original).

Men and women clearly have individual assignments, individual responsibility for personal salvation, and equal value. Yet they are inseparably, positively, supportively, and joyously bound together, that one whole unit may emerge to the fulfillment of the Lord's purposes and to our own glory. Such is our challenge— a challenge Satan was sure he could cause to be rejected or dismissed, but one the Lord knew we could meet. It is the challenge for which we came to earth, and the one that determines our eternal destiny.

CHAPTER 15

THE PLAN IS CALLED HAPPINESS: GRAB ALL YOU CAN

A n old saying suggests, "When you die, God and the angels will hold you accountable for all the pleasures you were allowed in life that you denied yourself." God assures us, "Men are, that they might have joy" (2 Nephi 2:25), and teaches us that we are designed to search after and enter into deep and meaningful relationships (see, for example, D&C 132:19–20). It is in these relationships that we will find true and everlasting happiness. Many who understand this principle are saying: "If that's true, why is it sometimes so hard?"

One of the few "sitcoms" I have ever watched (and I saw this one in late-night reruns) is titled *Mad about You.* It is a humorous and insightful exploration of the routines of married life by a couple who have fun, communicate, fuss, and fail; who care and hold one another precious; all amidst a flurry of activity. In one particular episode things in their marriage are not going so well. Jamie, the wife, quizzically says to Paul, the husband, "I don't know why this is so hard. It was supposed to be different." I suppose we've all felt that way at times.

Elder Neal A. Maxwell asked: "Why should it surprise us that life's most demanding tests as well as life's most significant opportunities for growth usually occur within marriage and the family? How can revolving door relationships, by contrast, be a real test of our capacity to love?" (*We Will Prove Them Herewith,* 9). Still, most couples are surprised when they discover that—contrary to the ideals of romance novels or the heady confidence they felt in the first blush of married love— blending two lives is filled with unique and life-altering challenges. If they're paying attention, they learn very quickly that keeping the joy in marriage is a building process. Let's do a quick recap and explore some last-minute reminders that will help you build toward that happiness.

Becoming Master Builders

The Savior, whom we would recognize as the "Master Builder," teaches us that we are all works in process, as are our relationships. But by building on his foundation, using his words as model and example, all things are possible. Building a marriage is not unlike other construction projects. There has to be a blueprint (your joint vision). The foundation is laid (your eternal commitments, with all the attendant principles and practices). Once the framework is in place, the bricks of a home or of a marriage are put in place one by one, no matter what your timetable.

After the "newly in love" stage is over and you enter the "growing in love" phase, building your marriage is like dealing with the flurry of details involved in building a home. Within the framework you've constructed, you must now set about finding a common ground as to the finishing details.

Think of each new challenge as similar to the common agreement you might make on the flooring, the tiles, the cabinets, the appliances, and on and on. Recognize that in looking at models and samples, examining and thinking carefully about what will work best, your discussions will be about likes and dislikes, about compromise, and finally about agreement over what will create a harmonious and beautiful environment.

Both partners need to accept that it is normal in this process for frustrations to arise and conflict to occur. If you've ever built or remodeled a house, you know this is true. And marriage is a never-ending building project. You will always be adding new wings, updating, and refining.

Both partners need to accept that it is normal in this process for frustrations to arise and conflict to occur. If you've ever built or remodeled a house, you know this is true. And marriage is a never-ending building project.

Living That Love You're Building

A friend told me, "Once you get the etiquette of marriage down, the rest is easier." That is important insight, for etiquette is nothing more than a sensitive awareness of the feelings of others. If something offends the other, don't do it, whether it is at a State Dinner or dinner with the family.

This sensitivity, this etiquette, is evident as exceptional love stories are played out. We have noted that each partner tries to bring freshness into the life of the other. They seem always to be looking for a way to lighten the other's load, a "treasure" to bring home, a new insight, a funny story, a phrase in a piece of music that's touched their soul, tickets to something they may not want to see but know the other does, a perfect apple, a single rose. They want to share together and to be together, as much as possible. They worry when their "other" is gone too long, or is carrying too heavy a burden. And they end each day with talk and gestures of love and prayer together.

But all that doesn't happen overnight. It takes time and careful attention to the finer details and a refusal to let the flames of that kind of love die. I was recently in the office of a friend who had these words racing across the screen saver of his computer: "I love [and he had entered the full name of his wife]." This kind of ever-present reminder of where and with whom your commitments lie can do much to stir positive thoughts in your mind. So can a photo of your husband in a prominent place in your work space. So can fun pictures, evocative of moments that belong uniquely to you together and to your family, in his workplace. Such images provide another important reminder of who you are, why you're together, and why what you share is worth fighting for and worth living for.

We are reminded by Anais Nin that love dies only when the work of keeping it alive ceases. "Love never dies of a natural death . . . it dies because we don't know how to replenish its source, it dies of blindness and errors and betrayals. It dies of illness and wounds; it dies of weariness, of withering, of tarnishing." Don't let that happen to your love!

Next comes the soul-building phase. Here's where the joys and triumphs of your life together are interspersed with the real work of keeping things fixed up and cleaned up. Neither love nor houses will stay forever new. Both have to be tended to, repaired, and ofttimes added on to. If neglect has gone on too long, entire areas have to be rebuilt. If the damage caused by the fires and storms of life has been too great, you may have to go back to the basics and build anew. Partnership love is an ongoing, exhilarating, exhausting, frustrating, rewarding building exercise.

Keep Your Ear Tuned to "Relationship Consequences"

My friend Cyndi is not only a gifted musician but an expert piano tuner, something she can do in her own time frame to help augment the family income. I admire this ability and asked whether this occupation was all about natural talent, or a perfect ear, or if there were something else at work. She said that both of those gifts are important, but you also must learn and adhere to the basics. You must keep trying to hear and hone that ear, and work very, very hard at paying attention to the slightest nuance. All must be combined if you are to bring a piano into perfect tune and thereby have an instrument on which beautiful music can be created.

I think creating beautiful marriages requires many of those same skills. Few people go into marriage with a "perfect ear," but by paying attention to the basics and being sensitively attuned to the subtle nuances, you can make your marriage call forth beautiful symphonies, great jazz, comic operas, and glorious hymns of praise. Let's look again at three relationship basics:

1. Be Available

Be sensitive, curious, listening and complimentary. Remember, one of the traits listed in my surveys as most desired by men and women was a mate who was available, who asked about them and really listened to their answers, who made them feel liked and loved.

We noted that men hear most clearly when the words used are concise, directional, or manly. Tell him that he's uniquely capable, that he's 100 percent correct. Compliment him on making the hard decision, taking the high road, or winning the day.

With sincere interest, ask him about the reason the earth stays in its orbit or how the layers of the earth came together. (I've learned so much from my husband about the makeup of the earth and the heavens as we've traveled—and it has made me enjoy the natural wonders of the world so much more and has kept him engaged and sharing during long drives.) Inquire about his favorite sports star and then really listen to what he says about things. When he's dressed for going out, suggest that you like the way his clothes set off his manliness.

And men, pay similar attention to your wives. Ask what they're thinking—and then listen. As we've discussed, women's brains are configured in such a way that they are always thinking about something, whereas with men's linear brains a lot of the time they aren't thinking about relationships. This means that, as a man, you will need to make a conscious effort to be attuned to your wife's thought process. Start by complimenting your wife and meaning it. In case you've forgotten, women need specifics and reference to details; the broad brush doesn't work that well for them. Talk about how her dress sets off her figure, how her skin glows, how divine she smells.

You know by now that women need to talk about relationships and feelings. Ask about a friend, a mother, the children—and listen. Ask for her advice on a matter you're both dealing with—and listen. Ask for her insight on a spiritual matter—and listen. Listening sincerely and placing real value on a woman's voice is a real "biggie," and the greatest compliment you can pay to her. Speak to her in her language, just as it is important that she speak to you in yours.

2. Be Fully Engaged and Adaptable

Live in the moment. Tease, flirt, be clever and fun. Look into his face; laugh at his jokes even though you may have heard them many times before. Men, turn off the cell phone and the Blackberry, put down the TV control or the game console, and engage. Women, turn off your concerns for connectedness with everyone. Stop multitasking, tune out the children, hang up the phone.

Be aware of each other's presence at all times. A daughter of a beloved father told me: "We always knew when Mother entered the room because Daddy changed. He became totally aware of her—totally sensitive to where she was and what she needed from him and from us. We still counted, but not quite as much."

Marriages work best when you don't demand but find delight in all the aspects of giving, when you don't withdraw but reach out in wonderful, affirmative, and optimistic ways. And this applies to the lovemaking aspects of your relationship as well. Look for ways to support both of your needs for romantic love.

According to scientific studies, romantic love for many women (not all) is about 75 percent in the head and 25 percent in the physical. It is just the opposite for the man: 75 percent in the physical and 25 percent in the head (and that was for nearly all men). Men, the time you spend romancing your wife will do amazing things for you—not just for her. Get romantic—not just physical—if you want a great love connection.

Women, you'll find more satisfaction in the physical if you daydream about your husband, plan surprises for him, get excited about remembering his touch and his words. Lead with the head; the heart will follow. Planning wonderful rendezvous—especially in your own space—will bring excitement to you, perhaps more than to him. Take turns setting the mood lighting—putting on the music—planning the treats you'll bring. He'll love that you cared and are available, and you'll love that the mood is so much like your "vision" of how lovemaking should be—and then it will become that.

Above all, eliminate from your life the three greatest relationship destroyers: withdrawal, contempt-based criticism, and defensiveness. Neither party can live with those. A rule of thumb for relationships suggests that we should be certain to have at least four positive exchanges for every negative one. Do your own counting and see how you do.

3. Put the Measuring Tape Away

We looked at "measuring" as one of the many reasons listed for unhappiness in marriage. Such measuring moves one's thinking over into the "unrealistic expectation" column, where happiness is seldom found. Who is this mysterious person that your partner doesn't measure up against?

Have you ever heard generalizations like this? "My doctor [my bishop, my co-worker—you fill in the general category] must be a perfect husband; he *always* has time for me, he listens with care to what I'm saying, and he has such wise and considered counsel." One unhappy woman said to me: "Before I married I had a great boss. We were on the same wavelength and *never* disagreed about anything." Men, take note—as these examples show, women love unity and communication. In fact, a woman most often measures your love in terms of time, listening, and valuable consideration placed on her thought process.

Conversely, a man may say in his head, "My co-worker has a great figure and we laugh at the same things," or "The woman I saw at the conference was dressed the way I wish my wife would dress," or "I see how my friend's wife treats him; it's like he's really terrific. That's how I would like to be treated." Women, take note—men tend to measure things in visual terms; they also like to be treated as the hero and made to feel clever and bright and wonderful.

President Gordon B. Hinckley spoke of this dissatisfaction to a group of young women: "Years ago I would interview many couple missionaries in the pursuit of my Church assignments. I would ask a missionary, 'What quality do you see in your companion that you would like to have in your own life?' There was usually a surprised look and a long pause. The individual had never thought of that question. He or she may have seen the faults in the companion but had failed to look for the virtues" ("Wonderful Thing That Is You," 6).

Find delight in your partner. Quit processing everything negative he or she does—look instead for all the positive things. Clear the other "ideals" out of your imagination. Let your partner emerge fresh and new. If you'll do this, you will remember anew that this is the one who makes your heart sing when you hear his or her footsteps, who knows and finds charming your little idiosyncrasies, who in sickness brings you soup and holds your hand, and who in health goes with you on delightful outings where you can plant just one more "memory rose."

Allow yourself once again to be vulnerable to your partner's love and need, to your own love and your own needs. Marriage really is about happiness.

You will remember that this is the one whose laughter you love to hear, whose worries or sorrows tear at your heart, and whose absence leaves an aching until he or she returns. Allow yourself once again to be vulnerable to your partner's love and need, to your own love and your own needs. Marriage really is about happiness.

And So We Arrive at the Ending

These, then, are the key truths about relationships. They are all about understanding who we are, placing value on the things that we do well together as well as on our differences, and supporting and giving voice in ways that both resonate and communicate.

Let me leave you with a few key points we have discussed during this journey together:

- See, value, and treat your partner as a hero or as a queen.
- Remember why you fell in love, what was and is wonderful and magical about your partner.
- Abandon criticism and disappointment. Don't allow unmet needs and unrealistic expectations to sabotage your marriage.

- Develop a plan, a common vision, and keep that vision intact.
- Keep the love alive, do things together, find joy in being a couple.
- Never stop growing as an individual within that partnership.
- Support and aid one another in both home and Church callings.
- Attend to your spiritual needs as individuals, as a couple, and as a family. Go to church together, attend the temple together, pray together—use your priesthood powers to bless and sustain.
- Talk—talk—talk with each other, about big things, small things, feelings, desires, hopes, dreams, and about just nothing.
- Express your gratitude moment by moment, your love day by day.
- Make God a partner in your marriage, in all your comings and goings, in your joys and your sorrows, your triumphs and your tragedies.
- Above all, keep your eye on the promise and the prize. "If a man marry a wife by my word . . . and by the new and everlasting covenant, and it is sealed unto them by the Holy Spirit of promise . . . [they] shall inherit thrones, kingdoms, principalities, . . . powers [and] dominions" (D&C 132:19). Never forget that by divine design you have been created to be heroes and queens. Be that to each other, be that for yourself, be that for your God.

Sources

Allday, Erin. "Men Gab Just As Much As Women." *San Francisco Chronicle*, July 5, 2007.

Aschkenasy, Nehama. *Eve's Journey: Feminine Images in Hebraic Literary Tradition*. Philadelphia: University of Pennsylvania, 1986.

Baron-Cohen, Simon. "They Just Can't Help It." *Guardian*, April 17, 2003.

Bennett, William J. *The Book of Virtues: A Treasury of Great Moral Stories*. New York: Simon and Schuster, 1993.

"Blame the 'Love Molecule' When the Passion Dies." *WTOPnews.com*, November 30, 2005.

Campbell, Beverly. *Eve and the Choice Made in Eden*. Salt Lake City: Deseret Book, 2003.

Christofferson, D. Todd. "Let Us Be Men." *Ensign*, November 2006.

Dahl, Larry E., and Donald Q. Cannon, eds. *Encyclopedia of Joseph Smith's Teachings*. Salt Lake City: Bookcraft, 1997.

Dowd, Maureen. "Genetically Speaking, Women Are Complex and Men Are Simpletons." *New York Times* News Service.

"Family: A Proclamation to the World, The." Salt Lake City: The Church of Jesus Christ of Latter-day Saints, 1995.

Faust, James E. "The Highest Place of Honor." *Ensign*, May 1988.

Flook, Maria. *More*, June 2005.

Freedman, R. David. "Woman: A Power Equal to Man." *Biblical Archeological Review* 9, January-February 1983.

Grant, Heber J. *Gospel Standards*. Compiled by G. Homer Durham. Salt Lake City: Deseret Book, 1981.

Hales, Dianne. "The Female Brain." *Ladies' Home Journal*, May 1998.

Hinckley, Gordon B. "First Presidency Message: Inspirational Thoughts." *Ensign*, February 2007.

———. "Ten Gifts from the Lord." *Ensign*, November 1985.

———. "To the Women of the Church." *Ensign*, November 2003.

———. "Women of the Church," *Ensign*, November 1996.

———. *The Wonderful Thing That Is You*. Pamphlet. Salt Lake City: The Church of Jesus Christ of Latter-day Saints, 1988.

Hymns of The Church of Jesus Christ of Latter-day Saints. Salt Lake City: The Church of Jesus Christ of Latter-day Saints, 1985.

Kimball, Spencer W. *My Beloved Sisters*. Salt Lake City: Deseret Book, 1979.

Liberman, Mark. "The Female Brain." *Boston Globe*, September 24, 2006.

Maxwell, Neal A. *Deposition of a Disciple*. Salt Lake City: Deseret Book, 1976.

———. *We Will Prove Them Herewith*. Salt Lake City: Deseret Book, 1982.

McConkie, Bruce R. "Christ and the Creation." *Ensign*, June 1982.

———. "Eve and the Fall." In *Woman*. Salt Lake City: Deseret Book, 1979.

McKie, Robin. "So Men's Brains Are Bigger." *The Observer*, July 17, 2005.

Moore, Thomas. *Soul Mates: Honoring the Mysteries of Love and Relationship*. New York, Harpercollins, 1994.

Oaks, Dallin H. "The Great Plan of Happiness." *Ensign*, November 1993.

Packer, Boyd K. "A Tribute to Women." *Ensign,* July 1989.

Perry, L. Tom. "An Elect Lady." *Ensign,* May 1995.

Saint-Exupéry, Antoine de. *The Little Prince.* New York: Harvest Books, 2000.

Smith, Joseph Fielding. *Answers to Gospel Questions.* 5 vols. Salt Lake City: Deseret Book, 1957–66.

Weaver, Sarah Jane. "Shared Religion." *Church News,* October 21, 2006, 7.

Widtsoe, John A. *Evidences and Reconciliations.* Arranged by G. Homer Durham. Salt Lake City: Bookcraft, 1960.

Wirthlin, Joseph B. "The Virtue of Kindness." *Ensign,* May 2005.

INDEX

~